RJD Publishing

UNBURDENED
BY THE
PROBLEMS
OF
SUCCESS

RJ Dalgliesh

A Trilogy

Book One

Unburdened by the Problems of

Success

Dedicated to my wife Kathleen who, after telling me that I have so many stories I should write them down, kept me motivated and inspired with love, encouragement and support.

ISBN-13 978-1537399591

First Edition

Content

Chapter

Chapter 1

The Horse

S he screamed "YOU BASTARDS! I BET IT'S NOT EVEN YOUR HORSE."

Let me take you back to the beginning of the story.

Myself, my best friend Ronnie and three other young guys lived in a large cottage on the outskirts of Edinburgh. Originally a farmhouse, it was in an idyllic setting surrounded by woods and fields yet close to the things we held most dear; pubs and beaches.

From our cottage there was a small dirt track that led down to the river. There it met up with a wide footpath which ran along the banks of the river for several miles. At that point a small humpback bridge crossed over the river and the footpath followed a gentle slope up through the woods and emptied by a fenced meadow. Running along the front side of the meadow was a small country road that ran for six or seven miles and led back to the outskirts of the city. On warm, summer weekends, this quiet little road was popular with walkers and picnickers.

The sole occupant of the meadow was a horse. This horse Henry, was a truly magnificent creature. He was jet black with a flowing mane, very soft sensitive eyes and four white patches above each of his ankles. Henry was the undisputed King of the meadow.

As I mentioned, we lived in a cottage that was formerly a farmhouse. In the yard was an old barn and in that barn was an Allis-Chalmers Model B tractor manufactured in the '40s. Ronnie and I took a real fancy to the tractor and with the limited mechanical skills we had, set about trying to make the tractor run. After a few hours' work and much cussing and swearing, the tractor suddenly leapt into life. This was more a tribute to the fine engineering of the Allis Chalmers company than anything to do the two numbskulls who floundered around trying to figure out how to make it start.

Having gotten the tractor running we now had to decide what to do with it. We had no fields to plow nor harvests to reap and certainly no cartloads of turnips to take to the market. After a few minutes' deliberation we decided why not just take it on a run up the river. So with one in the driver's seat and the other perched precariously on the back we set out on our maiden run. This was an undoubted success, we made it all the way to the meadow and there we met with a lot of curiosity from our friend Henry the horse.

On the way to the meadow we did meet with some startled stares and the occasional "What the hell are you doing?" from our fellow travelers on the path. We thought that perhaps we should install a horn on the tractor (which we fondly referred to as Alice) to warn people of our progress. However, we realized that with the rattling of the chassis, coughing of the engine and the occasional backfiring of the exhaust, everyone we met on the path was well aware of our presence long before we were aware of theirs.

We really enjoyed our voyages up the river to meet with Henry. We used to bring him sugar lumps, corn and some sweet grass we could pick from the opposite side of his fence. Henry became very close and he would always trot over to greet us as soon as we emerged from the woods astride Alice.

Now let me tell you an interesting little fact about Henry and his owner. His owner was a girlfriend, or at that point ex-girlfriend, of mine. Her father had bought Henry as a gift for her. Unfortunately, Henry bit this unfortunate young lady on one of her breasts. To me this was quite amusing as he had left perfectly square tooth mark scars on the top and bottom of her left breast. I'm not sure, but I think my levity towards her encounter with a mammary fixated equine contributed towards the premature ending of our relationship. I also think that perhaps I should have not mentioned this down the pub in the presence of both her and a bunch of my friends.

Here is a little bit of history about Henry. Henry was a retired racehorse. He did not have a distinguished career on the track, hence his retirement in a quiet meadow as opposed to being put out to stud. Like all thoroughbred racehorses Henry was quite highly strung. My ex-girlfriend found it almost impossible to ride him. In fact, it was almost impossible to even get on him. To do anything at all required an experienced team of handlers to distract Henry while the rider mounted. Once the rider became successfully ensconced on his back Henry could then be released. For the next five minutes it became the absolute prerequisite of the "holy shit why did I agree to do this" rider to try and stop Henry. Because of these characteristics Henry now led a quiet life undisturbed by the feel of a saddle or the crack of the whip.

One warm summer day Ronnie and I took a trip on Alice to see how Henry was doing. There had been some hostility from the Anorak wearers on the Riverside trail so we had now taken to wearing matching light blue sleeveless shirts and matching caps to give the impression we were somehow officials using the tractor to do some important trailside work.

We left the tractor at the end of the trail where it exits onto the country road and walked down the road till we were halfway along the meadow. Henry came across to greet us and we were passing the time by giving him some sugar lumps and sweet grass.

A young couple came by walking hand-in-hand enjoying a pleasant weekend stroll in the fresh country air. They stopped to admire the horse and strike up a conversation. "Is that your horse?" said the man in an accent that revealed he was from the other side of the city.

Feeling pride of ownership and knowing that we were the only regular visitors to Henry I replied "yes he is."

"What's his name?" asked the woman.

"Henry!" I proudly declared.

"He looks very tame. Do you ride him very often?"

I was unsure how to reply so I said, truthfully "as often as I can."

"Can I feed him one of your sugar cubes?" asked the man.

"Sure" I replied "it'll make you one of his best friends."

"Oh give me one of the cubes too" stated the woman. "I want to be his friend as well."

They both fed Henry sugar cubes and stroked his forelock. Henry was enjoying himself immensely with all this attention. I think he was remembering his halcyon days in the stables. Then things took a strange twist.

"I think I'll have a wee shot oh riding him," stated the woman.

Startled by the statement, my first instinct was to say 'you must be mad' but upon further reflection I thought I would try reason. "He doesn't have a saddle or bridle on and this would make it quite difficult for you to stay on him."

"Nae problem" said the woman "he's got a fine broad back and a great big mane, I could hold onto the mane and ride him nae bother."

I looked at Ronnie and he just smiled and shrugged. I could tell what he was thinking (it had been a while since Henry had had a good run.)

"Have you had any experience riding horses?" I asked the woman.

"Plenty" she stated emphatically "Portobello Beach is very close to where we live, and I have been riding the horses on that beach since I was a wee girl."

"I've seen her doing it" said the man, "there has never been a hint of her falling off, always in complete control. She rides the sands like she was born to it."

Now, I am very familiar with Portobello Beach. Located on the far side of the city, Portobello is a town sporting a mile-long front on a tidal estuary called the Firth of Forth. The estuary itself is over 10 miles wide and empties into the North Sea.

The seafront at Portobello contains a very nice beach and a stout seawall. Atop the seawall is a long group of businesses comprising of cafés, arcades, fish and chip shops, souvenir shops, fortune tellers, bed and breakfast establishments and an amusement park. It is a typical boardwalk-style seafront.

The horses the woman was alluding to were kept on the beach and for a small fee you could ride one. The prowess of the woman on these thoroughbreds, as attested by her companion, gave me more than some mild amusement. You see, the horses were not actually horses but some very tame donkeys which were led around in a circle by a handler. This, as far as I could make out, was her entire equestrian experience.

My rumination was interrupted by a "what about it then?" exclamation from the woman.

"Go on, she can't do any harm. That is a great big horse and he sure looks like he can look after himself," joined in the man.

At that point the discussion took a new turn. From behind me came "Ooh! What a bonny horse."

I turned to see a group of Sunday walkers, consisting of four women.

"I don't think he wants me to ride the horse" said the original woman.

"Why not?" said one of the women in the group. "It's a perfect day to ride around yon field on a nice horse like that."

"Come on" piped in another woman from the group "don't be a spoilsport, let her ride the horse."

Outnumbered, I decided to let the woman ride Henry. "Okay you can do it" I said with a bit of mischievousness in my heart. "If you can get on him then you can take him for a ride."

"Great!" said the woman, and the new group burst into applause.

I went over to Henry and patted him on the neck and said "Looks like you are going to have a passenger today old boy."

Henry looked quite nonplussed.

"Okay" said the man taking charge, "come on Bessie let's get you on the horse. I think if these two chaps keep feeding Henry you can climb up the fence and then swing onto his back; he won't even know you're there."

'Bessie', I thought. Well at least I know her name. It will come in handy later on for the police or ambulance report. Possibly both.

I said "Bessie, when you get on remember to lean forward and grip Henry's mane firmly." At this point I glanced towards Alice and thought 'I wonder how much petrol we have in the tank'.

Ronnie and I stood with Henry distracting him with sugar cubes and some corn. Bessie, with assistance from the man, started to climb the fence. The new group gathered around giving encouragement. The fence was fairly typical for the area. There were four strands of wire each about 10 inches apart. Holding on to the top wire Bessie stepped on to the lowest wire. The man took one of her arms and two of the woman from the new group took her other arm. With her feet swaying on the wire Bessie stepped onto the second wire. Now, unable to hold on to the top wire, Bessie let go and was supported by the man and the two women. She stepped onto the third wire and the group holding her could only reach her waist.

"You're high enough that you can swing your leg over the top wire and onto the horse," said the man. "Do it quickly, because once you go over the fence we're going to have to let you go."

"Ahm ready" said Bessie. "It's not easy swaying on these bloody wires. Here I go."

With a display of dexterity Bessie swung her leg over the top of Henry's back, grabbed his mane, and pulled her other leg over the fence.

Ronnie and I, standing with Henry and feeding him corn, got the first glimpse of what was to come. Henry's eyes popped wide open and started to bulge out. His nose flared and his mouth curled up displaying that fine set of breast chewing teeth. It seemed that Bessie started to say something which sounded like the beginning of "giddy up" but unfortunately she was drowned out by one of the loudest whinnies anyone has ever heard.

Fearing that Henry may jump straight over the fence we stepped back a couple of paces, but jumping over that fence was the furthest thing from Henry's mind. He reached back slightly, with every muscle tensed and showing, then he took off like it was the start of Royal Ascot. It briefly crossed my mind that if he had done this when he was racing he probably would not have ended up in this meadow.

Henry shot down the meadow at full gallop accompanied by the screams of poor Bessie which began to diminish the further away she got from us. I turned to look at the group of horse fanciers who were standing together wide-eyed and slack-jawed gaping at the rapidly diminishing sight of Bessie.

"What the hell!" said the man as he gradually recovered his sensibilities.

"I've never seen him do that before" I said. "Do you think she could have a burr stuck on her trouser leg?"

"For Christ's sake how are you going to stop it" said one of the women in the group.

"He's pretty old" said Ronnie. "He will probably run out of steam pretty soon," he added encouragingly.

By this time, at full gallop, Henry was approaching the top corner of the meadow.

"He's not a steeplechaser" I said "so he will probably turn rather than jump the fence. By God she's doing a great job of hanging on."

Bessie was indeed doing everything she could do to hang on. She had both arms wrapped around Henry's neck. As Henry made the turn at the top of the meadow we could see her right leg sticking straight down to prevent her rolling off of Henry's left side. Unfortunately, this was to no avail. As Henry swept at full gallop into a sharp right-hand turn, it became a slow motion movie as we watched Bessie's legs rise into the air and her arms start to gradually slide from Henry's neck.

The top of the meadow takes a shallow dip down from the fence. On the other side of the fence is a field that also slopes down into this gully. The road embankment is the third side and between them they create a natural draining point. During periods of extended rain a small pond can be created at this junction. However, it being summer, and unusual for Scotland, we hadn't had rain for a week or two.

Bessie's arms finally parted ways with Henry's neck. She took full flight and with an ear piercing shriek gracefully disappeared over the lip of the gully. A partial second later it looked like a shell had hit a World War One trench as a great pile of mud flew into the air.

The group, momentarily stunned by the rapid turn of events, broke into action and started running up the road to where Bessie had last been seen. We, on the other hand while facing the top of the meadow started backing down the road.

We had gone a few yards when Bessie pulled herself over the lip of the gully. Her hair, face and clothes plastered with mud with only her eyes showing. She looked directly towards where we had now paused, took in a deep breath and with all her might roared "YOU BASTARDS!"

The group stopped its run towards Bessie and turned to face us. We stood there arms open and shaking our heads giving the impression we had no idea how this could have occurred. The group resumed its sprint towards Bessie who was clambering to her feet apparently unhurt. We continued our innocuous backwards march towards Alice.

Bessie continued her tirade "I'LL BET IT'S NOT EVEN YOUR HORSE" she yelled as she slopped towards the fence mud dripping everywhere. "YOU SHOULD HAVE TOLD ME HE NEEDED A SADDLE!"

I thought that a saddle wouldn't have done any good even if we had nailed her to it.

By this time we had reached Alice and, joy of joys, she started on the second try. We mounted her and I turned to look at the day trippers, who now, led by a mud dripping Bessie, had started a determined march towards us, eyes full of malevolence.

We put Alice in gear and she coughed and clattered her way down the path towards the woods. I glanced over to the meadow where Henry stood placidly, the proud King of all he surveyed.

Alice started to put a good distance between us and our pursuers. As we entered the wood I said to Ronnie "I don't think the donkeys on Portobello beach will be making much more money off of Bessie."

Chapter 2

The Dog

We enjoyed living in the cottage because it really catered to our needs. Its location next to the main road going into Edinburgh made it easy to get to our jobs.

But, there were three bigger reasons to live there.

From our yard we could climb up a steep embankment that abutted onto a four-lane highway. Directly across that highway was the Cramond Brig Hotel, an old coach-staging inn. It was charming with two large bars and an excellent restaurant.

The second reason was the four-lane had a sidewalk. About three quarters of a mile walk up the highway was the Barnton Hotel. A large old hotel located next to the Royal Burgess golf club, reputed to be the oldest golf course in the world. Our interest in the golf was zero. The Barnton had two fine bars and a restaurant.

Finally, when you go from our yard down to the river and follow it north for about two miles it empties into the Firth of Forth. On this estuary is a village called Cramond. Small and very old it boasts the excavations of a Roman fort dating to about 100

A.D., a Kirk dating back 700 years and a small yacht club.

I do not want to get into a travelogue about the village of Cramond. Our only purpose for taking this walk was because the village contained an old and very homely pub called the Cramond Inn.

On a Saturday lunchtime, Ronnie and I were making our way back from the Cramond Brig. As we descended the embankment we could see something was at the front door of the cottage. As we got closer it's outline told us it was a dog. When we got to the very low wall that surrounded the cottage the dog noticed us and stood up.

"Ronnie, it appears to be tied to our front door handle."

"Oh yeah I forgot" he replied "that must be Jean MacDonald's dog, I agreed to look after it while she's away on two weeks' vacation."

We started up the path towards the front door and the dog, now fully alert, was glowering at us. When I say glowering, this animal brought glowering to a terrifying new level. He was a black lab unlike any black lab I had ever seen. A large head, glossy coat, shoulders a bodybuilder would be proud of and rippling muscles on his hindquarters.

A few feet from him was a bag of dog food and a dog bowl. Also taped to our front door was an envelope.

We approached the dog and a low lumbering growl came from him. Suddenly the dog, teeth bared and roaring lunged forward. Fortunately, the length and strength of the leash saved us. It stopped it dead and almost catapulted it backwards. It then went into a furor of growling barking and snapping.

We beat a tactical retreat.

"With another lunge like that, the beast is liable to rip the handle right out of the door and whoever it's most pissed off with is in deep trouble" I said. "Perhaps we should go back to the Brig and consider the situation."

"If we feed it, it will know we're friendly and that might change his demeanor."

"How are we going to feed it?" I said, "if we get anywhere near it it's liable to rip our arms off."

"I'll do it," said Ronnie," we just need a plan."

"I'll stay out front, if you go around the side and then come round the corner and sidle along the front of the cottage I will try and distract it while you get the food."

"Okay" said Ronnie, "let's do it."

He headed around the side of the cottage, and I stood at the end of the path looking at the dog who was now sitting staring at me. Quite a few minutes passed with no sign of Ronnie. I was beginning to wonder if he had chosen the first plan and gone back to the Brig. A couple of minutes later his head appeared around the corner of the cottage and he nodded to me.

I started waving my hands in the air and shouting "Hey! Hey! Hey!" I thought about shouting "Come and get me you big brute," but I didn't want to risk it maybe understanding English.

Ronnie stepped around the corner of the cottage and I noticed with some bewilderment that he was wearing a pair of elbow length, leather Welder's gloves. Where in God's acres he had come up with these I had no idea.

Keeping close to the wall of the cottage he started stealthily moving along the front. This was noticed instantly by the beast. It turned towards him and went back to its low growling mode. To his credit he kept going and realizing that the beast had him fully in his sights started talking softly to it. For some reason this seemed to work and the beast did not go into full berserk mode. He was able to reach the food without an attack being launched. He emptied some food into the bowl and pushed it forwards. The dog started to eat. He picked up the second bowl went around the corner and came back with a bowl of water. The dog seemed quite grateful.

Ronnie scratched the dog's head, played with his ears and gave him the full chorus of "good boy, good boy."

Finally, it looked like we were going to be able to get into the cottage.

Ronnie un-taped the envelope from the front door and took a look inside.

"His name is Bruce and we have all his care instructions in here."

Untying Bruce's leash from the front handle the pair came walking down the path towards me. I tentatively let Bruce sniff my hand and then scratched him behind the ears.

A band of brothers had been formed.

We didn't know it at the time but Bruce was going to prove to be a very different kind of a dog.

We spent the afternoon with Bruce throwing him sticks, taking him down to the river, and going up through the woods so he could meet Henry.

As evening approached we prepared to spend Saturday night at the Brig.

"What should we do with Bruce?" Ronnie asked.

"We can just leave him in the cottage, I'll betcha we don't get burglarized."

"Good idea, let's go."

We spent a few hours in the Brig and at closing time headed back down to the cottage. By now it was quite dark.

When we got there, our three roommates were standing at the end of the front path.

"You guys had better watch out" said Ted "something has gotten into the cottage."

"I tried to open the front door" added Jim "and it came rushing down the hall, sounding like a wounded Minotaur, I barely got the door closed."

"We've tried looking through the windows" said Alec. "We see a sort of dark shadow prowling around but can't make it out."

"I did" said Ted. "I was at the window and it came straight at me, it's eyes were glowing red, I thought it was going to come flying through the glass."

It's only Bruce" said Ronnie. "He's a black lab I'm looking after for his owner."

"Who's his owner," said Jim, "Lucifer?"

"You must be the only two who can go into the Cramond Brig and exit with the hound of the Baskervilles" added Alec.

"He's a nice black lab" I said. "He just doesn't know us all yet."

Ronnie went up to the door to unlock it; the others started shuffling backwards across the yard. When Ronnie opened the door there was a cacophony of barking but it stopped abruptly when Bruce recognized who it was.

With Ronnie having Bruce under control the rest of us trooped into the sitting room. Ronnie brought Bruce in and each of the guys began to introduce themselves. Bruce seemed okay with this. We poured some beer into his bowl and Bruce lapped it up. He was now officially one of the crew.

The only uncomfortable person appeared to be Alec who said, "I hope you two are taking that dog into your room and keeping the door closed, because if I get up during the night I don't want to run into the satanic puppy."

"It'll be fine" we said, "we'll keep him nice and close." After a while we all retired to our rooms and peace settled over the cottage.

The next morning Ronnie and I were going into Edinburgh and didn't think it would be a good idea to bring Bruce with us. We also did not want to leave him alone in the cottage based on the near calamity the night before. After some deliberation, we decided to put him in the barn. It seemed like the best option. It gave him plenty of room, lots of light and he was safely behind two very stout barn doors. So, with Bruce firmly ensconced in the barn complete with food and water we set off for the city.

A few hours later we returned and were surprised to see Bruce sitting on our front doorstep.

"Hey boy" said Ronnie as we walked up the path." Who let you out of the barn?"

"I think you should take a look at the barn" I said.

Ronnie turned, his jaw dropped and all he could say was "Holy shit!"

As I mentioned, the barn had two very stout doors. But now, it had two very stout doors which in the bottom center had a gaping hole. Half in one door and half in the other.

We went over to the doors to take a look. The hole was surrounded by teeth and claw marks.

"Do you think the landlord is going to notice this?" said Ronnie.

"Not if we park the tractor in front of it, but he may wonder about that."

"We could say a wild animal must have done it" said Ronnie. "The zoo is fairly close, we could tell him something escaped from the zoo."

I pondered this for a moment. Edinburgh has one of the largest zoos in the world. "That might work."

"If he wants to phone the zoo to find out if there has been an escape, we tell him they always lie about it because they don't want to alarm the community" added Ronnie.

"A wild animal getting in or out is probably our best option." I said "no one is going to believe a dog could have done this."

"In any matter he's not here that often" said Ronnie. "The day he sees the damage we say that we just noticed it ourselves and were about to give the zoo a call. We didn't want to go into the barn itself in case whatever did it is still there. That should put us in the clear."

I nodded, but then took a look at Bruce. "If Bruce is here, we better keep him out of sight."

We decided that we should keep Bruce with us at all times. This should prevent any more mishaps. The nice thing about Scotland is dogs are welcome in almost every pub. One evening we decided to take a walk up to the Barnton Hotel. The Barnton is a railway station hotel built in the late 1800s. The station is long gone but the hotel retains the Victorian architecture and ambience of the era. It contains two bars. One is called the Public bar. You would consider this a downscale gathering place. Noisy, sawdust on the floor, sit on a stool by the window or stand at the bar.

The other bar is called the lounge. It is much more upscale with carpeting, tables with upholstered chairs, velvet patterned wallpaper, designs etched in the windows and a civil bar staff. Slightly more expensive than the public bar but much more relaxing. The lounge was where we were headed.

I sat at a table with Bruce while Ronnie went up to the bar to get us a couple of pints. In the area of the lounge where we were in, the tables were close together and arranged in a horseshoe shape. We were sitting by a window at the top of the horseshoe crescent. The place was busy and Bruce lay on the floor keeping a watchful eye on the activity. As the tables around us filled up no one seemed to notice or even care that Bruce was there.

A couple of our friends joined us. Then surprisingly my ex girl-friend and one of her girlfriends showed up. Everything was going well and even my ex seemed glad to see me. (I made a mental note not to mention anything about bite marks)

Tony, one of the guys sitting with us asked "When did you get a dog?"

"It's not our dog" said Ronnie." We're looking after it while the MacDonalds are on vacation."

"That's not Jean MacDonald's dog is it?" said Tony.

"Aye" said Ronnie quizzically.

"Are you sure she's coming back for it?" chimed in Ray, "I hear the dog has something against women."

I had to defend Bruce "Ach, yer all full of it, he's as gentle as a lamb."

At that point a bar patron wearing a tweed jacket, bunnet on his head, puffing a pipe, pint of beer in his hand and faithful dog by his side came strolling over and sat down at a table on the end of the horseshoe.

Conversation at tables in our area began to cease as a low grumbling growl began to intensify. As it got louder the reverberation started glasses rattling on the tables. People stared at us and finally noticed Bruce as he slowly raised up out of the shadows, glower on his face and hackle hair standing on end. I got a tight grip on his leash and Ronnie grabbed his collar. The two of us were praying we could hold him. I caught the new patron's eye, he gave me a nod, stood up and he and his dog walked around the corner to an unseen table. Having saved the immediate community from this danger, Bruce relaxed and lay back down.

"Is that dog safe?" came a plea from another table.

He's as gentle as a lamb" said Ray while looking at us, "Just don't let any women or dogs come near him."

"You could probably add barn doors to that list," said Ronnie under his breath.

The evening continued and things seemed to be re-kindling with my ex-girlfriend. Fortunately, nothing about her horse entered our discussion. Ronnie was also getting on well with her friend. As was the law in Scotland, closing time in the pub was at 10 o'clock. We emptied out into the parking lot but the night was still young. I was standing outside holding Bruce and talking to my ex. She said he seemed a lovely dog and reached over to pat his head.

That's when Bruce bit her.

It wasn't a snarling bite, more of a just don't touch me little nip. I looked at her hand. He hadn't gone through the skin at all.

Before I could stop myself I said "It's just some tooth mark indentations."

She snatched her hand back, gave me a withering look and said, "You just won't change!"

Undaunted, and with the bravado of youth, I said, "Would you and your friend like to come back to our cottage?"

"Are you and your dog crazy!"

She walked over to her friend who was talking to Ronnie, hooked her arm, and the two of them stalked off.

Ronnie came over to me and asked "What went wrong?"

"Bruce screwed it up, let's go home."

The next morning it was just Bruce and I in the cottage. Outside was very pleasant, clear blue skies, windless and warm. I decided to take Bruce for a walk down to the river to Cramond Village. There he could have a run on the beach.

It was a poignant day as Bruce's owners were coming to pick him up tomorrow. This would make it the last chance I would have to take him on a good walk.

The route we took led us across the highway to the Cramond Brig. Behind the hotel is a small road that leads down to the original bridge (Brig) across the river. This is a narrow, three arch, stone bridge dating from the 1600s. (What did they know about building bridges 400 years ago we don't know now?)

Across the bridge we made a left onto a path called the Almond River walk. This walk led into a gorge that had been formed by the river over the centuries. There were fairly high, treed bluffs on both sides of the river and the walk was cut into the right-hand bank.

We were pretty much alone during the walk with just the occasional angler wearing waders standing in the river. After about a mile and a half we came to the Cramond weir. This is a remnant of bygone days when a mill stood next to the river. Partial ruins of the mill still exist by the waterfall – a very picturesque part of the walk and on busy days many people pose here for pictures. A little further on the walk opens up into a flat grassy expanse perhaps 50 feet wide and 175 feet long. It lies at the foot of a small road called the Old Mill Brae. People like to sit in this area picnicking and admiring the river.

The walk narrows again until you reach the beginning of the small harbor at Cramond Village. The first thing you come upon is the yacht club.

Because this is a tidal estuary and the Almond River is fairly narrow the yachts and boats are mainly small, day sailers. Beyond the yacht club is an ice cream parlor followed by a few houses. At the end of the houses is a road swinging to the right and going up the hill. Close to the foot of this road was our initial destination the Cramond Inn. It was just past lunch time so we went into the bar for a pint and a couple of meat pies. It was very quiet and there were no incidents involving Bruce. He was a picture of placidity.

After our break, we exited back down to the river estuary. The river Almond empties into the Firth of Forth which is probably four or five miles wide at that point. There is a wide circular paved promenade and a paved walkway heading along the shore of the Forth for several miles to another beach area known as Silverknowes. Looking out onto the Forth there is an island, also called Cramond, about three quarters of a mile from where we stood. When the tide is out you can easily walk over to the island. Fortunately, when Bruce and I arrived at the beach the tide was fully in. We walked down the ramp to the sand and I let Bruce off his leash. We had the place to ourselves.

Bruce initially was running up and down the beach. I started to grab some driftwood sticks and throwing them for him to fetch. After a little while I started throwing the sticks as far as I could out into the water. Bruce gleefully jumped in, swam out to the sticks and brought them back.

Then something happened that I have never seen before or since.

Another fellow walked down to the beach with his dog. Light brown in color not too much smaller than Bruce it was a good-looking athletic dog. Bruce, still intent on his retrieval games, gave it no heed whatsoever.

The man moved some yards up the beach from us and began to look for a nice piece of driftwood to throw for his dog. I threw Bruce's stick far out into the water and Bruce took off after it. A few seconds later the other guy who had found a stick threw it out into the water for his dog. Both Bruce and the other dog retrieved their respective sticks at about the same time. To my great surprise Bruce started swimming towards the other dog. He grabbed the other dog's stick in his mouth and wrenched it free, Bruce then started swimming back to shore with both sticks followed closely by the other dog.

The dog's owner standing on the shore just stared at me. Bruce arrived and deposited both sticks, I handed the other dog's stick to his owner.

"That's unbelievable" said the guy "I've never seen a dog do that before, what came over him?"

"He must've thought your dog was in trouble and came over to help out, he's a rescue dog you know."

"A water rescue dog" said the owner incredulously, "whatever am I going to see next."

"Next time I'll have him wear his Red Cross harness."

Not sure what Bruce's next move might be I said "well, we have to go, enjoy the rest of your afternoon on the beach."

Bruce and I walked back up the ramp, I put his leash on and we headed back the way we came. After we passed the yacht club and were back on the path I unclipped Bruce's leash so he could get more of a run. He trotted on ahead and in a few minutes disappeared behind some bushes onto the grassy plain.

I rounded the bushes and immediately saw that trouble was brewing, in fact it had already brewed. Standing there was a girl who was staring at Bruce and Bruce in turn was staring at her dog whom he had obviously backed into the river.

The girl turned to look at me, and although I did not know her very well I did recognize her. Alec, our roommate knew her much better than I did but to help you follow along with our ensuing conversation I will give you a few facts. She lived fairly close to the Barnton hotel, she was also a member of the equestrian set, she knew my ex-girlfriend and had gone to a local and very exclusive private girls' college.

This college Ronnie and I referred to as our 'Happy Hunting Ground.'

There was a slight flicker of recognition in her eyes as she said, "That damned brute has forced my dog into the river."

"Bruce" I called as I walked over and snapped his leash on.

Now there was full recognition on her face "I might have known it was your dog!"

This haughty slight of my faithful, although temporary companion, irked me.

"Aha!", I exclaimed "all that noise I heard last night was the rhythmic beating of the jungle telegram tom-toms."

"You're damned right, frightening people so they can't get into their room at night, going to the Barnton hotel and freaking customers out so they had to leave without finishing their drinks and then taking your dog out into the parking lot so he could go around biting people."

"I recognize you now, sorry I hadn't seen you without your jodhpurs and hardhat, where's your riding crop? Probably next to your broom."

"Why you... If... You... I'll... You... When I..."

"My Lord, the proud owner of a private education and can't even form a proper sentence."

"Where's your friend?" she finally blurted out, "You two are never seen apart, is he lurking around somewhere?"

"On Friday afternoons he leads the singing at the Christian Outreach Center."

"There's no Christian Outreach Center around here." she said scathingly.

"It may be Greek Orthodox or Catholic I'm not exactly sure which."

During this exchange I had been standing with Bruce attached to his leash but I had not moved Bruce from the spot where he had been menacing the other dog. Because of this the other dog was still standing in the river.

At that point the man I had met down at the beach came walking around the bushes. "Hello again" he said cheerily. "A good day for dog lovers."

"This woman's dog is in the river trying to commit suicide," I said to him. "I can't say I really blame it, my dog is trying to coax it out."

Going nearly apoplectic the woman choked out "You damn liar, your dog chased him in there."

"That's a rescue dog," said the man "I witnessed him down on the beach helping my dog."

I took Bruce a few steps away from the riverbank, knelt down and called to the other dog,

"Come on boy, out you come, it's all right I'm here now."

Her dog duly came trotting out of the river.

"There you are" said the man to her "he's quite safe now, boy, don't they make a good team."

He gave a wave and a "Cheerio" and happily headed up the Mill Brae.

Her face was purple, her entire body trembled and it looked she like she was going to swallow her tongue.

"Now that's over" I said, "Do you fancy going down to the Cramond Inn for a pint. I was there earlier, very quiet. It'll give us a chance to get to know each other better."

She was standing there staring at the man going up the hill oblivious to what I had just said. "Rescue team" she muttered. "Mayhem by them up and down this river" pause, "rescue team??"

It began to dawn on me that this was going nowhere. "Come on Bruce let's go home."

After we had walked some yards I turned to wave goodbye. She was standing there affixed to the spot, staring at us. Her look reminded me of a couple of lines from a Robert Burns poem.

Gathering her brows like a gathering storm,

Nursing her wrath to keep it warm

Chapter 3

The Road

There came a time when I had to think about starting a career. When in high school I was very adept at technical drawing. I could slice and dice any kind of an object and show all elevations on a plan.

I decided to use these skills to become an architect. After a bit of searching I went to work for a firm that was designing an American-style mall in the center of the city. My title was Apprentice Architect. This was a large firm with offices in various cities but the main attraction for me, now that I was living at home, was I could walk to work in under 10 minutes.

A couple of days after I started working for the firm I was called down to the Chief Partners office. His office was guarded by an anteroom in which sat two administrative assistants. One of whom I had met previously when I came in for the job interview. Her face was permanently painted like a Cheyenne Indian on the warpath and she possessed all the charm and personality of Grendel from Beowulf. The other admin was similarly painted but the artist had added a smile on her face, much more pleasant.

Grendel said to me "just wait there."

"Do you know what this is about?"

"You'll find out soon enough," hissed Grendel.

I stood there wondering if Grendel liked living at the bottom of a pond.

A few minutes later the pleasant admin's phone rang and she said to me "go on in."

When I entered the Chief Partner was sitting at his desk with two men sitting off to the side.

He asked me to sit on the chair in front of his desk and said "this is Detective Wilson and Detective James. We have had a rather unpleasant incident and they would like to ask you a few questions."

"Do you know where the petty cash is kept?" asked Detective Wilson.

"I've only been here two days and as yet I can barely find my way to my office."

"Someone stole the petty cash" said Detective James.

"I would have no idea where to begin looking; in fact, I had no clue that petty cash was even kept in the building."

"Well, I reckon you can go" said the Chief Partner.

As I headed up to my office I thought to myself "quite an auspicious start to a new career. If I were them I would start with a bright light and a rubber hose on Grendel."

Things settled down after that incident but I found the work not to be very demanding. I was in charge of designing the toilets in the anchor store and making sure that the stairways had the correct risers and elevations. This was done mainly through the use of stencils. I had little stairway stencils, little toilet seat stencils, gentleman's piscina stencils and bathroom sink stencils.

To become certified as an architect I not only had to perform an apprenticeship with the firm, but I also had to attend university. Edinburgh had many great technical colleges but in their wisdom someone decided that these architecture classes would be best served by the University of Edinburgh Art College.

Most of the classes I found to be interesting. They focused around design and construction. But being an art college there were some less than technical classes thrown into the curriculum. These were drawing and painting. I am an awful free hander and an even worse painter. My trepidation at attending these classes proved to be well warranted.

My art professor had some weird fixation about painting pictures of fruit in a bowl. An apple, a banana, and a pear seemed to be to be his favorite choices. Still life he called it. Our first class gathered and after an introduction from the professor everyone got their paints out and sat down at an easel viciously studying the fruit in the bowl.

I started to paint the fruit but after a few minutes I realized this was going nowhere. I ripped off my first attempt and started on a fresh sheet. I thought I would do my own interpretation. This consisted of painting a blue sky at the top of the paper and green grass at the bottom. In the blank portion between the sky and the grass I painted a couple of trees, one an apple tree, the other a pear tree. I also included the sun, a horse and a black dog. High school was so boring I learned to look busy but all I was doing was doodling. I had developed a pretty good rendition of Fred Flintstone so I added him to the painting.

The professor was going round the class giving advice to the students. When it became my turn he just stood behind me silently looking at my painting.

After a while he said "This has got nothing to do with the class assignment."

"I tried doing the class assignment sir, but I just can't paint."

"Then how did you ever get into art college?"

"I'm in the architecture program."

"Aha" he said as he nodded knowingly. "You just carry on doing the best you can."

Now this wasn't all bad. We had classes studying the human form using live models. Most of these classes involved sketching naked women. I really tried hard and I think this is where I did some of my best work. My classmates tended to get annoyed because from my seat in front and center I would keep offering suggestions to the model for some athletic new poses.

Life at college was good but the majority of my time was spent at work. Our offices were located in a part of the city known as the New Town. When I say New Town I mean the area was constructed between 1750 and 1850 consisting of large four-story townhouses designed for the wealthy of Edinburgh and really meant to last. They had wide cobbled streets and circuses which on both sides curved around a communal private garden. A few of them had been converted into offices although strict regulations meant absolutely no reconstruction to the outside and limited reconstruction on the inside.

Our offices were located on one of the circuses. When you entered through the front door you could look up and see all the way to the fourth floor where my team was located. The mezzanine required walking up a curved stairway passing along a straight portion that had the mezzanine on the left and the various doors for the drawing rooms on the right and then onto the next curved stairway. This configuration continued all the way to the fourth floor. Each of the office areas had teams consisting of five or six architects and technicians led by their lead architect. I was never quite sure but I think we had about six or seven teams in the building.

The team on the third floor was an enigma. No one actually knew what they were working on and their lead architect was one of the shadiest persons you could ever meet. Whereas the dress in the entire office was fairly relaxed, this man turned up every day with a Brooks Brothers three-piece suit, shirt and shoes and a carnation in his lapel. No one had ever seen him do any work or direct any of his team in doing their work. He used to move stealthily around the building staying in the shadows as much as possible and never conversing.

Unfortunately, it fell to my lot, that one day he started a conversation with me.

From now on I will refer to him as Mr. Shady.

I was returning to the office one afternoon after having been at class. As I made my way up the stairs there on the third floor landing was Mr. Shady.

As I walked towards him he turned to me and said "Ah RJ, I hear you're doing very well."

I was dumbfounded.

He continued "This project is getting very close to the construction stage, the demolition is complete and the site clearance and leveling is nearing completion. They're going to be driving foundations very soon."

My dumbfoundedness was now replaced by a certain suspicion about my new found friend.

"There is one very important task that has to be completed" he continued "I think you are the very man for the job; I'll speak to the Chief Partner and see if I can have it assigned to you."

"What would that job be?" I asked hesitantly.

"There is a service road that runs underneath which gives delivery access to all units that are contained in the complex. The path of the road has been determined but we need someone to contour it."

I knew very well what a contour was. In my days with the Boy Scouts we had very detailed maps we used when we went hiking. The contour lines followed the slope of the hills and the closer they were together the steeper the slope. But, these hills, valleys and mountains had been designed by God, I wasn't sure how I could improve on the Lord's work.

"I haven't contoured a road before, are you sure you would like me to do this?"

"You'll pick it up in no time at all, I'll make the arrangements to get all the drawings to you."

At that point Mr. Shady slipped back into the shadows.

I continued up to our drawing offices and once there told our lead architect what had happened.

"Looks like you were in the wrong place at the wrong time. He has a history of doing this, it lets him squirm out of what he should be doing. Unfortunately, for some unknown reason he is the Chief Partners Golden Boy and has his ear."

I went back to my drawing board and sat there looking at my T-square and my little stencils thinking to myself, "What the hell just happened?"

When I got to the office the next morning sitting on my drawing board were some new plans that hadn't been there when I left the previous evening. With a feeling of dread, I popped them out of their cardboard sleeves and when I spread them open, there in all their glory, were the plans for the service road.

The most detailed one showed the service road laid over the initial site. This also had all the original height elevations and contour lines. The simplest plan however, showed the service road after the site had been leveled. This was my favorite plan because it occurred to me that all the leveling had been done and there was nothing else for me to do. But to be sure, I needed to check with the civil engineers on the site.

This required me to make a phone call. In order to make that call I would have to get an outside line. To get an outside line you called our switchboard operator. Unfortunately, that switchboard operator was Grendel. All the members of staff below the rank of lead architect hated doing this because whenever you asked for an outside line an inquisition started about who and where you were phoning. I thought I could get around this by charming Grendel. I picked up the phone.

"Hi there, hope you're doing well, you looked great last time I saw you."

"What do you want?" she hissed.

"Nothing much, oh by the way Bandersnatch and the Harpies are playing at the Palais de Danse tomorrow night, I have a couple of tickets do you fancy going."

The hiss lowered a couple of octaves "what do you want?"

"Oh, just an outside line."

Brrrrr

I called the civil engineering firm and got put through to Angus McKay the lead engineer on our project. I explained to him the task I had been given and proffered the opinion that since the site had already been leveled my additional work would not be necessary.

"You want to put a flat and level road underneath and all around that size of a building?" he asked.

"I thought it would be the easiest and quickest way to get the road completed."

"You idiot have you never heard of rain? It is something we occasionally get here in Scotland. In order to build a road you have to camber it, put in gutters and lay drainage pipes into the sewer system. We normally design and contour the road but you bunch of wankers sitting in your ivory tower decided that you would do the contouring. There was some fancy bugger from your office with a flower in his lapel prancing around the site the other day. We listened to him for a few minutes and then told him to fuck off."

I now knew why I was hand-picked to complete the contouring of the road.

"Angus, if I understand you properly my job is only to give you a plan with the contours on it and you will take it from there adding all the drainage etc.?"

"Do you inky-fingered dolts never talk to each other? Why in hell's name would an architectural firm be doing all that civil engineering work? Just get me the contour plan as soon as possible."

"Angus, so far you have called me an idiot, a wanker and an inky-fingered dolt. To me it seems these insults are coming from a gormless highland pratt who spends all day farting around in sewers and drains. It looks like you didn't have the brains to get yourself out of the gutter."

There was a bunch of spluttering coming from the other end of the telephone line. "Wha dae yi think yer taalking to?" said Angus reverting into his native Highland dialect, "Why don't you come over here and tell me this to my face."

"I think if I got anywhere close to your face the smell of cheap whiskey would probably put me on my back."

"I'll be the one who puts you on your back."

I know you're probably missing your favorite sheep Angus, but I'm not having sex with you."

"You smart mouthed prick, I've a good mind to come over there and sort you out."

"You come anywhere close to my office and I'll kick you from one end of Queen Street to the other." A good mile by the way.

"That's it! I'll be there in five minutes; what's your name?"

I thought quickly, gave him Mr. Shady's name and added "I'll be waiting."

Click.

I hung up the phone and looked up, all my colleagues were sitting at their drawing boards staring at me.

"We should look out the windows," I said to them, "things could get interesting."

We gathered around the windows and in less than three minutes a van bearing the civil engineering firm name came skidding around the cobbles on the corner. It screeched to a halt at our office door and the vans' front door flew open. Out stepped a movie stereotype for a Highlander – a large man with bright red hair bright red beard and a bright red face. He should've been wearing a kilt and carrying a battle ax in one hand and a Claymore in the other. He looked around, stared at our front door, then strode up the steps.

Almost immediately a great roaring came up from the vestibule. It's intensity grew as it got louder and louder. We stepped out of our office onto the landing leaned over the banister and stared down to the ground floor. There we saw a very unusual site.

Angus was standing at the foot of the stairs and Grendel was standing two steps up so she could stare him in the face.

"Get oot ah mah way wuman" roared Angus "ahm goin' up there to find that wee bastard and knock him seven ways sideways!"

"The only place you're going" hissed Grendel "is Intensive Care at the Royal Infirmary."

By now the ruckus had brought everyone out onto their landings. They were gathered at the banisters staring down at the unlikely matchup. Angus looked up at the crowd and said "Is this an architectural firm or is it Cellblock H?"

Grendel stared straight at Angus and I could swear I saw two lines of dark blue daggers going straight into Angus's face. "You have a choice," came the hiss "Do you want to walk or get carried out of here?" I noticed that although Grendel had her arms down, her hands were now in the shape of claws and her nails looked like barbed steel. If Angus takes one step forward he's going to have some real damage done to him.

This unexpected challenge seemed to knock the bluster out of Angus. Grendel took one step down and Angus took two steps back. "I'm no done" said Angus "I'll find him." Angus then swung around and marched out our front entrance.

I went back to my drawing board sat back in my chair and thought to myself, "Well that didn't go so well." My initial plan had been that after the phone call I would go down to their offices and take a look at a few plans of completed service roads. With Angus being somewhat angry I now discounted that maneuver.

But I did have a plan B. I would go to the City Planners office and look at a few of the plans which contained similar roads in similar projects.

The next day after art class I took a five-minute walk over to the City Planners office. At the front desk I explained my dilemma to a not unattractive young lady. Her attitude put the civil back in civil engineering. She was completing her degree in civil engineering at Herriot-Watt University and understood exactly what I needed. She took me back to the stacks and started pulling drawings that were very relevant to my task. We spent the rest of the day going over these drawings and by the time I left her I had a pretty clear idea of how to do the project.

The next morning I sat down with the plans and began to get busy. The road was shaped like a capital Q with two tails. The inlet road went down the side of the building and then curved underneath as it went by each of the loading bay doors. As it circled around there were a couple of small bends until it emerged from the other side of the building it then made sharp 90° turn to parallel the inlet road and exited to the street.

I started putting the contour lines on the drawing. After a while I thought to myself this road looks exactly like a racetrack, in fact, with the road outside the building disappearing into a tunnel and then exiting the building, it's almost like the tunnel section of the Monaco Grand Prix F1 racetrack.

With this in mind, I started to bank the corners and the two small bends. For the 90° turn coming out of the building I gave it the largest amount of banking I thought I could get away with. When I was finished I sat back to admire my work. You could drive around this at 120 miles an hour no problem at all.

With an air of finality, I rolled up the drawing and put it in its tube to send over to the civil engineers. Screw Angus and Mr. Shady, the delivery drivers are going to love this.

Chapter 4

Musselburgh

Musselburgh is a town, proudly named after a shellfish, that lies 6 miles east of the center of Edinburgh. To get there you travel through the coastal towns of Leith and Portobello. You then traverse the river Esk. There are two bridges crossing the river. One built by the Romans at the beginning of the first millennium; this is referred to as the old bridge. The other bridge was built in 1806; this is referred to as the new bridge.

Ronnie had moved into a flat on the High Street in the dead center of town. It was located next to the Old Tollbooth on what was once a market square. It was an ideal location for several reasons. It sat on the main road to Edinburgh and therefore had a regular bus service in and out of the city. Across the road was a fish & chip shop and directly below his flat was a pub.

One Saturday night we decided to go downstairs to the pub. The place was raucous with a mixture of people of all ages. We managed to burrow our way to the bar and claim some ideal space next to the beer taps.

We had been there a while when two young ladies managed to break through the crush and make some space next to us. Ronnie immediately went into pick-up mode and offered to buy their drinks. This offer they graciously accepted.

Their names were Rhonda and Jill; they found it quite amusing to be talking to the two Ronnies. As the evening progressed and the drinks flowed everyone became quite amiable. Inevitably they went to the bathroom as a pair.

Ronnie turned to me and said, "Mine is Rhonda."

"What do you mean yours is Rhonda? She's the good-looking one. I don't know what line Jill was in when God was giving out looks, but whatever it was, she must have been standing at the back of it."

"Remember the pair we picked up at Cramond College, I did you a favor by taking the less attractive one; and I stuck it out all night so you could work your wiles on her friend. So now it's your turn."

I could see his logic. We normally did turnabout but always had this argument at the beginning.

"Okay" I said "I'll stay as long as I can manage it."

As was the law, they called last orders at 10 o'clock. This was followed by Ronnie enthusiastically telling the girls that his flat was just above the pub and we should go up there and drink a few more beers. To my dismay they both said yes. I was stuck because if I didn't go, the two of them would probably just leave.

We went up to his flat and cracked open some beer. Ronnie became firmly ensconced on the couch next to Rhonda. Jill and I sat next to each other on two chairs. Without the group interaction I was running out of things to talk to Jill about. Funnily enough, and I don't know how this came up, we had a mutual acquaintance in Flynn O'Rourke. Flynn and I had been friends for a long time and this gave me a chance to occupy some time by telling her about our band, the OrDal Quartet.

The quartet was quite unusual in so far as we only had two members. I played piano and Flynn played a small electric organ. We knew only one tune, a late 60s hit by the Mindbenders called "A Groovy Kind of Love." As we became more adept at playing the song, it became a race to see which one of us could finish it first. The OrDal Quartet had only one appearance before an audience, a local amateur talent show; incredibly we did not win.

The pauses in our conversation gradually began to lengthen. It finally boiled down to Jill asking me what I did for a living. I was going to answer apprentice architect but I was seriously bored with it and was considering a career change. In fact, when I was leaving the office on Friday afternoon Angus was standing in the vestibule in front of Mr. Shady. He was waving a drawing tube, which I could only assume contained the contoured drawing of the service road, and calling Mr. Shady a 'feckless idiot'. Mr. Shady had taken full credit for the design and quick delivery of the drawing so he was in no position to deny his involvement. As I stepped through the front door there was a redeeming factor which brought a smile to my face.

The last words I heard Angus shout were "You could race the Indy bloody 500 around it."

I had a friend Jerry Hutton who was a hairdresser. Whenever he told a girl this, it seemed to inspire her into endless conversation. So I told Jill that I was a hairdresser. She immediately launched into talk about shampoos, conditioners, gels and sprays.

At that point, with Ronnie's help, things took a dark turn.

"I'm really in need of a trim "said Jill.

Ronnie, who's interest in our conversation had suddenly been raised chimed in with "why don't you give her a quick cut."

"That would be very nice" added Jill.

"I don't have any of my stuff."

"No problem, we have very good scissors in the kitchen and I'll find a comb."

"Great, tell me where you keep your scissors and I'll go get them while you find a comb" said Jill.

"Just sit tight, I'll get everything" said Ronnie.

This seemed to seal the deal. I thought I would flounce around like a real hairdresser and snip the scissors without actually doing anything.

Ronnie gave me the scissors and a comb and Jill sat up in her chair with a towel around her shoulders.

I stood behind her flipping her hair with my hands and asked her "Is there any particular style you had in mind?"

"It's pretty dim in here so you can just give me a trim" she slurred in reply.

I started my haircutting act with the pretend snipping. After a little bit I thought "this looks pretty easy", so I started evening out her hair by cutting a little here and a little there. After a few cuts I realized this was a mistake, and to make matters worse, I started to fix my work.

A little while later I said "I'm done."

She stood up and with a slight stagger made her way over to the mirror above the fireplace. I stood next to her, blocking as much light as I could, and did my hair flipping routine.

"You have wonderful hair; you should become a hair model."

"It's very bonny" added Ronnie.

Jill seemed satisfied and staggered back to her chair. At that point I noticed that Rhonda was asleep, or passed out, on the couch.

"Well, I should be going before I miss the last bus" I said, "it was very nice to meet you Jill, give Rhonda my best."

"Very nice to meet you RJ, and thanks for the haircut."

Rapidly I made my exit.

Early next morning, as the good people of Musselburgh slumbered, there came from the market square a cacophony of banging, thumping and shouting. The events that follow are as Ronnie related them to me.

"I got up wondering what was going on at our front door. I opened it and thought some practical joker was playing a Halloween trick. Standing there was a ghoul with eyes like slits, mouth clenched and hair looking like a haystack had exploded. Then the specter screamed "WHERE IS HE!" As it pushed by I realized it was Jill."

The barrage continued "The last thing that RJ is, is a hairdresser!"

"Why do you say that?"

"Just look at my hair!"

"Different, but not bad. He's a very modern stylist."

"When I get a hold of him I'm going to stick those scissors up his arse."

She did a double take of the scissors sitting on the coffee table.

Picking them up she said "These aren't scissors, these are pinking shears."

"He did say he didn't have his stuff."

"No one in his right mind would use pinking shears to cut hair! Where does he live? I'm going over there right now and I'm taking these pinking shears with me."

"He just moved, I don't have his new address."

"Then where is his Salon? Me and these pinking shears are going to be waiting outside when he gets there tomorrow."

"He doesn't have a salon. He has a van and travels to his customers' houses."

"Even better! Give me his number and I'll make an appointment."

"I've no idea what his business number is."

"You're lying! Flynn O'Rourke knows him, I'll talk to Flynn and find out where that haircutting prick lives."

Later that day Ronnie and I met up in a pub in Edinburgh.

"You better get a hold of Flynn and warn him. I don't think anyone could be anymore pissed off but, if she finds out you are an architect, it could happen."

I called Flynn from the payphone and he almost choked with laughter. He told me that if she got in touch he would arrange to meet her just so he could see her hair.

"Everything all right with Flynn?"

"He hasn't heard from her. I don't understand why she would be so annoyed. It didn't cost her any money and there's only a week between a bad haircut and a good haircut."

"Good point. I'm seeing Rhonda tomorrow and I'll ask her to tell Jill that."

"You know, Musselburgh is now off-limits and every time I go through Portobello my head has to be on a swivel. I think I'm just going to stay within the confines of fortress Edinburgh."

Chapter 5

Shirts

As I was growing up there were two hobbies I was absolutely in love with; HO scale model railroads and electric slot cars. The railroad hobby has stuck with me until this day. The slot cars were with me until my early 20s at which point I had built a huge layout. As a teen I used to think "boy it would be great to work for the company that makes the slot car sets."

Bored with architecture, I had left it behind and was mulling about a different career. Casting an eye through the job ads in the newspaper one day, I froze when I saw an ad from the company that makes the model railroads and slot cars I had grown up with. They were looking for a trainee sales rep. I immediately sent a letter applying for the position. A few weeks later they replied and asked me to come for an interview. I met with the National Sales Director and the Scottish Regional Sales Manager. Somehow I managed to impress them, and a short time later I was offered the position. I was ecstatic.

The company's headquarters and manufacturing plant was located on the southeast coast of England. This is where our national sales conferences were held a couple of times a year. Annually there is a national toy show in Brighton, England which is attended by every manufacturer of toys in the UK and Europe. It also attracts all retailers of toys throughout the UK and many from Europe.

Prior to the show our entire sales force gathered for a meeting at company headquarters. This was basically to go over new products we would be showing and the strategy we would employ on our stand, which incidentally was the largest in the show. Our National Sales Director wanted each sales rep to wear a fresh white shirt every day. There were 35 reps so multiply that by four and the company would be buying 140 white shirts.

He then turned towards me and said "RJ, will you get everybody's size then go down to N&T's and buy the shirts."

I was shocked that he would offer this awesome responsibility to the most junior member of the team.

I went around the room methodically recording each person's neck and arm size but disregarding requests for Button-down collar's, French cuffs and Cufflinks.

With a blank check in hand I set off for N&T's.

N&T's is one of the largest retail chains in the UK. It has branches in almost every single town and multiple branches in the larger ones.

At the shirt counter the saleslady greeted me with a friendly "What can I do for you luv?"

"I need 140 white shirts."

"Do you now luv? We get enough jokers around here. You want me to call security?"

"I really do, I was sent here by the company I work for. Here is a list with all the sizes and here is a blank check from my company."

"I'm going to need some help and we will need to get a lot of this out of the stock room, this is going to take a little while luv."

"That's okay I'm in no hurry."

The really surprising thing was, they had all the shirts in the sizes we needed.

But the story doesn't end there. This was the 1970s' and retail computerization was still in its infant stages. N&T's headquarters had recently installed a computerized inventory control system.

Suddenly this Star in the Crown, white shirt sales award winning store, started receiving truckloads of white shirts. It took them weeks to stop them.

Chapter 6

Rock

Brighton sits on some sandy beaches on the south shore of England. It began its rise to prominence in the mid-to-late 1800s when a railroad was established between London and Brighton. During the Victorian era it was felt that drinking seawater and bathing in seawater helped all kinds of illnesses.

During the 1900s, prior to the advent of holidaymakers heading off for Spain, it enjoyed its glory years. Along the sea front are many large and small hotels. Because of this preponderance of accommodations it became a Mecca for conventions.

One of the things it is famous for is a candy called Brighton Rock. This was a solid cylinder of hard candy approximately 12 inches long and half inch to 1 inch in diameter. Pink on the outside, white on the inside it contained the name Brighton all the way through. So no matter where you broke it or bit into it; it still read the name Brighton.

Our company in the spirit of Brighton ordered I don't know how many thousand sticks of rock with the company name inside.

During the last day of the sales meeting the company unveiled this gift. It was to be handed out to customers during the show.

"RJ" the National Sales Director said, "since you're the only one with a company station wagon we would like you to transport this rock down to Brighton."

"Love to."

I just couldn't believe how many of these awesome responsibilities I was being handed.

"Well that's a wrap, everybody head for Brighton and we will see you at the hotel. RJ go and find the warehouse manager and they will load the rock."

First thing on my to-do list was to find out where the warehouse was. It was a little after five on a Monday and people were leaving to go home. I stopped a man coming down the corridor and asked him where I might find the warehouse.

He looked at his watch and said "You might not find anybody in there at this time mate."

"I have to pick up some items we're taking down to the toy show."

"If you follow this corridor straight down you'll come to a door that will let you into the factory; keep going straight until you get to the door on the far side. It will take you into a courtyard; you will see the warehouse on your right, the office door is the small red one."

I thanked him and started running down the corridor, through the door, through the factory, through the door onto the courtyard, sprinted to the red warehouse door and grabbed the handle. It was locked.

I'll need to find someone with a key I thought. As I was running through the factory I had noticed there were quite a few people still working. I went back into the factory and asked a person working at a bench where I could find the shift supervisor.

"She'll be up there," she said pointing to a bank of windows high on the wall on the far side of the factory.

I said thanks and headed towards the bank of windows. Once again through a door, up the stairs and there was a door marked supervisor. I knocked and a voice said, "Enter."

Sitting behind a desk, was I hoped the answer to my dilemma. I explained my problem to her and the necessity to get into the warehouse.

"The warehouse is a secure area; the keys are limited to the warehouse manager and his assistant."

"What if you ran out of parts during your shift and production would stop unless you got more parts from the warehouse?"

"In that case we'd talk to security who would let us in and record whatever we take out."

"Where would I find security?"

"If you go across the factory floor to the far right-hand corner there is a door, go through it and the second door on the right will say 'security'."

I thanked her and headed downstairs and onto the factory floor. "How many times do I have to trek across this bloody floor" I thought to myself.

I reached the security office, looked through the internal service window, no one was there. What now?

At that point a cleaning lady came down the corridor pushing her trolley. "Hello" I said with the friendliest smile I could muster, "Do you know where I might find the security guard?"

"Well pet, if he's not warming his arse in the office then he's on his rounds. He has to punch his key in the security boxes all over the complex. It's to make sure he is doing his job. Drives him bonkers."

"How long does it normally take?"

"I've no idea" she said looking through the service window, "but his thermos and lunch pail are sitting on his desk so he'll be back for his dinner."

"Thanks, I'll just wait here till he gets back."

"You're welcome pet, I hope it's not too long."

I sat down the floor, back against the wall, and began my wait.

About an hour and a half later I heard footsteps in the hallway. I stood up and there, approaching me, was a man in a uniform complete with peaked cap. I introduced myself and brought him up to date on the rock saga.

"I can't let you go rummaging around in the warehouse!"

"I'm not going to be rummaging around, a bunch of large boxes marked Brighton rock should not be difficult to spot."

"I still can't let you in there, besides it's my dinner time."

"The toy show is the biggest event of the year. They plan for it all year long. Every executive in the company is there and they write 70% of next year's business during this period. Unless I get that rock there on time there is going to be hell to pay."

I had no idea whether this was true or not but it was getting late and I had to get that rock into my car.

"Okay, I'll let you into the warehouse but I'm coming with you."

"Great! We'll get that rock loaded and I will be out of here."

Thus began the warehouse search. After an hour we had not located anything that remotely looked like boxes of Brighton rock.

"Well, that's that." Said the security guard.

"I need to call the warehouse manager," I said "Do you have a number for him?"

"It's gone 10 o'clock, you can't phone him at this time!"

"I'm going to have to call someone which means I have to start working my way up the chain of command. I reckon by the time I get to the end there is going to be an awful lot of annoyed management."

"Let's go back to my office and I will give you Paul's number."

Paul, I assumed was the warehouse manager.

Back at the office I was duly given the number and I gave Paul a call. He didn't seem concerned about being called at this time of night. I told him of my search for the elusive boxes of Brighton rock.

"We took them over to the conference center where they were having the sales meeting" he said.

I couldn't say anything.

After a few seconds of silence his voice came over the phone line, "Hello?"

"So, all the rock is in the conference center" I said into the phone while looking at the security guard.

"It sure is. They wanted to take it as soon as the sales meeting was over. We stacked it all by the back door."

"I'll get it loaded and on its way to Brighton" I said weakly "Thanks Paul."

I started the trek back to the conference center accompanied by the security guard. He opened up the rear door and there, neatly stacked in the Hall of Valhalla, was the mother lode.

"Okay, I'll get my car and we can get this loaded."

"I can't stay here loading rock into your car" said the guard. "It's time for me to do my rounds, I have to turn my key at each of the security stations between certain times. I've already missed my dinner hour."

"That's okay, I'll make sure I securely close the door when I leave."

The guard seemed torn about this but he nodded, said "good luck" and headed back to the factory. He left me with the feeling that he was kind of glad I was leaving.

I brought the car over and started loading the boxes. There were more boxes than I could fit in the station wagon so I had to open some boxes and stuff the individual packages of rock into any available space. After about 45 minutes I had all the boxes and packages of rock crammed into the car. It was almost midnight but finally, and happily, I was on my way to Brighton.

I didn't know it then, but my battles against bureaucracy were far from over.

I arrived in Brighton sometime after 2 AM. The conference center and our hotel were located on the boulevard which ran between the beach and the town. The boulevard was a brightly lit four-lane road with colored lights and decorations all the way along it. It was completely deserted. I was concentrating on looking for signs to the convention center when suddenly alongside me appeared a police car with flashing lights and a policeman waving me to stop.

I stopped, and as was the practice in those days, the police car pulled in front of me. Two policeman stepped out and approached my car. I rolled down my window and the one on my side asked me to step out of the car. I got out and noticed that another police car had pulled in behind.

"What's all that in your car?" the policeman asked.

"It's boxes of Brighton Rock."

"Where did you get it from?"

"I brought it with me."

"You brought boxes of Brighton rock to Brighton?" he queried rather incredulously. "Let me see your license."

I gave him my license and while he was looking at it I noticed there were two policeman standing at the rear of my car and one standing at the front. It seemed that a car driving down the Boulevard in the early hours of the morning was big news in Brighton.

"Why are you driving around with boxes of Brighton rock at this time of the morning?"

At this point I explained who I worked for and these were giveaways to our customers at the toy fair.

"What toy fair?"

"The one that starts in the Brighton Conference Center tomorrow."

"Do you have any proof that this rock belongs to you?"

I opened my wallet and pulled out a business card with my name and the company name on it. I then reached through the window of my car and grabbed a package of rock, opened it, and showed him the company name inscribed within the rock.

"I was late receiving the rock" I said "that's why I'm down here so late."

"It's fine" he said to the two policemen at the back of my car, "you can go."

"Before you go, let me give you some samples of the rock for your kids."

I grabbed three more packages and handed them around. They said thanks and got back in their cars and left. I'm sure even if they had any kids they would never see that rock.

I got back in my car and sat there for a few moments thinking "they have my registration number, they have my driving license number, they have my name and address and they know what company I work for. If tomorrow there are headlines reporting the great Brighton Rock Heist, I'm sure if they start an investigation, within the next 2 to 3 months I will be receiving a knock on my door."

I continued on following the signs for the Brighton conference center. Arriving I pulled up to the gate in front of the loading docks. This had a small security guard shack and a security guard stepped from it. "Oh no" I thought, "things aren't going to get any better."

"Can I help you Guvnor" he said.

"I hope so" I said cheerfully "I have a late delivery for the largest exhibitor in the show." I told him our company name which he instantly recognized and said he loved our products.

"Okay he said, there's still a lot of setup going on in there so just give me the delivery docket and I'll let you through."

"I actually work for the company so I don't have a delivery docket."

"No docket, no can do"

I handed him one of our rock packages and said "these are freebies we are handing out to our clients and I have to get them onto our stand."

"No docket, no can do."

I could see I was banging my head against a brick wall so I bade him good night and headed for our hotel. My plan was to get a few hours' sleep and sort everything out in the morning.

I arrived at our hotel which was situated on the Boulevard facing the beach and ocean, a venerable building dating back to the early 1900s. I was very glad to see it.

As is the custom in most of these hotels they lock up around midnight. I parked in front of the double entrance doors and walked up the steps looking for the Night Porter bell. I gave it a ring and waited. Nothing happened. I gave it a double ring and waited, still nothing. I peered in through the windows on the door; the reception area was all lit up but no sign of life. This time I gave it a triple ring and after a few seconds I saw a door opening behind reception.

The Night Porter emerged dressed in the typical Porter garb of gray trousers, black vest, white shirt and bow tie. He was a man probably in his mid-50s, slight paunch, receding hairline, gray hair and looking decidedly bleary eyed.

He came up to the door and pressed his head up against the glass cupping his eyes with his hands. "What do you want?" He shouted through the window.

"I want to get to my room" I shouted back.

"Who are you?"

I pressed a business card against the glass, he read it and then I heard the sound of the door unlocking.

"You must have had fun" he said "it's gone three in the morning."

"I'm just arriving in Brighton and believe me it's been no fun" I replied. "If you come down to my car with me we can get these boxes unloaded. Where would be the safest place to store them?"

He stared down at my heavily loaded car sitting at the bottom of the steps. Turning towards me he said "you can't bring all that in here!"

"I can't leave it out there in the car, it will all be stolen by the morning and after all the trouble

I've had to get the stuff down here I can't allow that to happen."

"We've nowhere to put it."

I was tired and getting towards the end of my rope dealing with obstructive people. "This vestibule is very large, you have double doors that can swing wide open and there are only two steps to get into the hotel. If you guide me I can back the car right in here."

"Are you stark raving mad? You can't bring a car into the lobby."

"Why not? I see them displayed in hotel lobbies all over the country." I had not seen any cars in any hotels but I had a vague recollection of seeing a picture in a magazine of a car in a very swanky hotel lobby.

"You're not displaying yours in this lobby tonight, and that's final."

Off to the right was the hotel bar, it had two glass doors and it was locked. It also had plenty of space so I said to the porter, "How about if we put the boxes in the bar, they will be safely locked up and we will have them out of here first thing in the morning."

"First of all, that is a bar and not a storage area, and secondly I am not carrying all these boxes into this hotel."

"You're a Porter aren't you?"

"I handle luggage; I don't handle freight."

I thought to myself, "Boy it's lucky Ronnie isn't here otherwise this guy would be hanging by his suspenders from the coat hooks."

I was running out of options. By using the elevator, it would take me well over an hour to unload the car and take the boxes to my room. Then I had a flash of inspiration.

By law in the UK, a resident of a hotel may request that the hotel bar be opened for them at any hour of any day. From what I could see through the glass doors there were comfortable sitting chairs by a large bay window; they looked directly down to my car.

Turning to the Porter I said "Please open the bar for me."

"What! Are you going to start drinking now?"

"No, I just want to sit in there."

"I can't open the bar just to let you sit in it."

"That's okay, I'll have a soda."

"The bar is where we sell beer and liquor, if you just want soda take a seat and I will serve you right here in the lobby."

Sitting in the bar with a beer in front of me was a risk I couldn't take. The hotel was full of our sales reps, sales managers and various department directors. It would not look good for them to come down to breakfast and see me unconscious in the bar with a drink in front of me. If the night Porter saw me asleep, he would most likely add a whisky next to my beer.

I gave the Porter a long unblinking look and said "I am going to be here for the rest of the week. If you have any sick or vacation time coming up I would suggest that you take it." I then walked out of the hotel.

I got back into my car and reclined the seat a quarter-inch, which was all the boxes would allow me. The Boulevard lights were still on and some early morning traffic was stirring. The waves beat on the shore and a gray light crept over the horizon. I lit a cigarette and as I gazed into the distance murmured "Rock, I think this is the beginning of a beautiful friendship."

Chapter 7

My Three Amigos

I have three very good friends I used to spend a lot of time with. They were Anton who worked in his father's garment factory, Rainer who owned a leisure center and Dick who was a sales exec in the souvenir industry.

We had a favorite pub where we would meet almost every Friday and Saturday night. The pub was called 'The World'. It was fairly new and resided on one of the narrow back streets in the center of Edinburgh.

It was designed with a traditional, but upscale, pub look. It had wood paneling, carpet and a six-sided mahogany L-shaped bar. The bar was divided into two levels by three steps between the lower and upper arms of the L. The design gave the bar six sides for seating and plenty of room to stand. It had a few tables on the lower level and stools at the bar. The upper level, on the other hand, had no stools or seats; it was standing room only. Our favorite spot was the upper-level. The three sides of the upper leg of the L, with the bar in between, gave us a clear view of everyone on our level. The five feet between each side of the bar and the wall made it very cozy when it became crowded.

This was very much of a pickup bar on the weekends with the clientele divided almost equally between young men and attractive ladies. We always stood in the same corner with one side of the bar in front of us and a short corridor which led to the three steps down to the lower-level behind us. Inevitably as the area filled up there would always be some young ladies either next to, or very close to us, plus we could always say hello to any of them coming up from the lower level. It was a very strategic position.

After several weekends at the pub, I noticed that Anton, Rainer and Dick, no matter how hard they tried, were getting nowhere with the female population in the bar. Also, when I was chatting to a female, they tended to muscle in and compete for the young lady's attention.

One Friday I decided that I would not get involved in the pickup fracas; I would stand back and enjoy watching the other three make all the moves. Little did I know I had struck gold.

During the evening two very attractive and unsuspecting female prospects, a blonde and a brunette, moved next to us and ordered drinks. With the presence of adjacent women, my friends instantly switched into wolf mode. After we introduced ourselves they began to employ our rich inventory of pick-up lines. This wasn't as bad as 'Did it hurt when you two angels fell from heaven?' or 'Apart from being sexy what do you girls do for a living' but it wasn't far off.

From my position, leaning against the wall while quietly drinking my beer, I could see this was beginning to go horribly wrong. It even took them a while to get their names, Mary and Jean, and I wasn't even sure those were their real names. As far as I could see, the only reason the two girls had not moved away from us was because the bar was packed and you couldn't go anywhere.

It was nearing closing time and the relentless chat up banter was now going at a frenetic pace. I was enjoying watching the whole spectacle, it gave me a whole new perspective on how we behaved on a weekly basis. I had noticed every now and again one or the other of the girls would glance towards me.

The call for 'Last Orders' came from the bar staff. My friends offered to buy the girls drinks. They declined, so the boys turned towards the bar to get their order in.

At this point the brunette turned to me and said "Is there something wrong with us?"

Taken by surprise I said "What do you mean?"

"You've leaned against the wall the whole time ignoring us."

"I'm sorry, I didn't mean to be impolite. I was just having a quiet evening."

"Why would you come here for a quiet evening, wouldn't you be better off at home with your slippers and a pipe?"

"You just stood there while your wally friends prattled on with their inane banter. You took no notice of us, do you think we're that plain?" chimed in the blonde.

By this time the boys had got their drinks and had turned around to see me being berated by two angry women. Holding true to form, and not wanting to squander all the goodwill they felt they had created, they stood back and let whatever was going to happen to me happen.

"I, I..."

"Have you any idea how long it took us to get ready to come out?" interrupted the brunette.

I took this as a rhetorical question but I was beginning to feel like a man with two wives. "I think you're both lovely. With looks like yours it couldn't have taken you hardly any time to get ready."

"What do you mean by that! You think we don't care how we look?" The blonde exclaimed.

"Absolutely not, I think you are the two most attractive women in the bar."

"Your aloof attitude certainly didn't demonstrate that."

"I suppose I'm a bit shy, it's not often I meet women as stunning as you two."

"Your friends didn't seem to be shy. My God the lines they came out with, they must sit at home and practice them all week."

"They're nice guys, just a bit awkward at times in front of new girls. Their hearts are in the right place."

"That's nice for you to say, but you didn't have to stand there and listen to them all evening." Pause "You think we're stunning?"

"I most certainly do!"

"Well thank you," continued the blonde "you're a pretty good-looking chap yourself. We were just a little bit put out by your attitude."

"Tell you what, just across the road is a little restaurant, well it's more of a hamburger joint, but it has a late wine serving license. If you want, we could meet there once I separate from my friends."

"Are you sure you'll come?" said the brunette.

"You can absolutely count on it. I want to make up for my poor attitude."

"Okay" said the blonde. "We'll see you there."

At that point my three amigos, seeing things had apparently settled down, rejoined the conversation.

"Are you ladies going on anywhere afterwards?" asked Anton.

"No, I think we'll just go home."

"That's a pity, maybe we'll see you here again."

"Maybe you will."

With the crowd now emptying out of the pub, the two girls said 'Cheerio' and left.

"That was close," said Rainer, "I hope we see them again."

"Well, nothing to do, so I'm off home." I said.

"Same with us," said my friends, "we'll catch up with you tomorrow night."

With that, we left the pub and headed in our various directions.

Once I felt that the coast was clear I doubled back and went into the little restaurant. Sitting at a table with a bottle of wine were Mary and Jean.

We had a wonderful time.

Saturday came, and at lunchtime I was in our local pub having a pint with Ronnie. He was now going steady with Rhonda, one of the girls we met in Musselburgh.

I opened with my usual question. "Is Jill still annoyed about the haircut."

"It's still tops her list of things that anger her. She hasn't stopped trying to find out where you live and keeps ranting on about the pinking shears. I think she has them in her purse. Every time Flynn sees her he brings up how awful she looked. He's even got people who never saw the hairstyle talking about it. It really sets her off. If I were you I would keep avoiding Musselburgh."

"I will. On another subject, I found out the strangest thing last night."

"What's that?" he asked.

"If you ignore women, they get very curious about why you're ignoring them. For some strange reason it seems to attract them. I've been thinking about it all morning and I just can't figure it out. Anyway, I'm making the 'World' my center of operations and I am going to start ignoring as many women as I can."

Chapter 8

The Auld Enemy

In 695 A.D. two tribes, the Picts and the Gaels united. This created the kingdom of Alba; Gaelic for Scotland.

Over the ensuing centuries many invasions of Scotland were made by the English and their allies, some successful and some disastrous. Throughout these troublesome times the fierce national pride of the Scots never diminished.

Although swords, spears and shields are now just relics of a bygone time, the rivalry with the English still exists in the form of soccer and rugby. These are sporting battles that rekindle in the hearts of many Scots, reminders of a past and proud independent nation.

The British Home Soccer (Fitba') Championship was an annual tournament from 1884 till 1984. The tournament comprised of England, Northern Ireland, Scotland and Wales.

During these 100 years the annual game between Scotland and the "Auld Enemy", England whipped the Scottish nation into a fervor.

One year it would be played at Hampden Park in Glasgow; the following year Wembley Stadium in London - and so on and so on.

I was sitting in our local pub with my friends Kelsey Moore and Reggie Macdowell when Harris Firkin, another friend of ours, came in.

Harris sat down at our table, said "Boys, do I have good news for you." He looked at us one at a time with a big smile on his face.

"Are you going to tell us?" questioned Kelsey.

"As soon as you buy me a pint."

I rose from the table went over to the bar and brought back the requested pint "Okay, let's hear it."

"Griffin called me from Hawick," began Harris.

Griffin Tompkinson was a member of our circle. He was currently working for Pringle Knitwear, a company based in Hawick, a small town in the Scottish Borders about 55 miles south of Edinburgh.

Harris continued, "Griffin said if we act quickly he can get us tickets to this year's Scotland vs. England Fitba' game, seats on a private coach to take us to London, and accommodations once we are there. To reserve the package all we have to do is send him the money and get to Hawick on the Friday night before the game."

"Sounds great!" said Reggie "When does the coach leave?"

"It leaves on Friday evening and drives overnight to London. It will drop us at the boarding house where we will stay after the game. On Sunday morning the coach drives us back to Hawick."

It was a unanimous yes, and as none of us had ever been to London, we were truly looking forward to the trip.

Chapter 9

The Auld Enemy – The Trip

We sent Griffin payment and on the designated Friday we all piled into Harris's car and headed down to Hawick. We picked up Griffin and he guided us to the parking lot where we would meet the coach. We were early, so we cracked open cans of beer and waited.

Our fellow passengers began to arrive; many of them from the pub across the road and followed our example. Soon it began to look like a small Scottish encampment. Everyone in Scottish dress varying from kilts, tartan trousers, tartan shawls, scarf's, flag shirts and an assortment of Scottish tams. It looked like it was going to be quite a weekend.

The coach pulled up, its side bore the company name and a large logo of a Scottish flag. The door opened with a hiss, the driver emerged and opened the luggage compartment. "You can load your luggage in here boys."

Everyone silently looked at each other. Finally, a self-appointed spokesman for the passengers said "What luggage?"

I then realized there was not a single female among the passengers.

Everyone got busy selecting seats and loading their beverages aboard. This took a while, but unlike modern air travel, everyone was in great spirits.

The driver closed the door and the coach pulled away from the curb. A great cheer went up from the fully loaded (in more ways than one) coach. One of the guys at the front of the coach stood up in the aisle and shouted "Let's get this trip started with a wee song!"

To the tune of Camptown Races, a melody we would all get very familiar with over the next two days, the passengers burst into:

London Wembley here we come

Doo-dah Doo-dah

London Wembley here we come

Doo-dah Doo-dah day.

The coach rumbled into the night accompanied by songs and the constant hiss of beer cans opening. A cacophony of boo's greeted our crossing of the English border. This was immediately followed by the driver stopping the coach after many passengers voiced a desperate need to relieve themselves by the roadside.

We reached our boarding house in London about 7 AM the following morning. We probably would have made it much earlier but the driver had to stop the coach every 30 to 40 minutes for the comfort of his passengers. We also had a late evening break for a meal at a diner. Unfortunately, the diner had an alcohol license and it took the driver a lot of time and great effort to get the coach reloaded.

Unencumbered by wives and sweethearts, the group was a rapidly regressing to their simian roots. Based on their behavior, you could put 'Lord of the Flies' into the non-fiction genre.

As we stood outside the boarding house Harris said "let's check in and leave the beer in our rooms."

We stood in line at the check-in, cases of beer cradled in our arms. The check-in was a hatch in the wall behind which the hotelier stood. A ledger on the shelf in front of him, and on the wall behind, a board full of keys hanging on hooks. He was checking off each guest's name in his ledger and handing out keys. It did not take long for our turn as many of our fellow travelers were still milling around outside, confused as to where they were and how they got there.

The check-in went as follows:

"Name."

"Dalgliesh."

"Room five, next."

"Tomkinson."

"Room five, next."

"It looks like Griffin and I are sharing." I thought.

"Moore."

"Room five, next."

"Firkin."

"Room five, next."

"Macdowell."

"Room five, next."

The five of us stood there looking at our room five keys.

"Do you think this place only has one giant room?" asked Griffin.

"Let's go take a look" I answered.

We headed up the staircase to the first landing and looked around the circular balustrade. Directly across from us was the fabled room five. We walked over to it and Kelsey opened the door.

We shuffled in as a tight group and were amazed at what we saw. The room was kind of dingy, but it was huge. There were five single beds arranged around three of the walls, but instead of butting up against each other, there was plenty of room between them. A large picture window gave lots of light and a perfect view to the street below. The fourth wall was where it all came together. In the center it had a fireplace with an electric heater, a couch on one side of the fireplace at a 90° angle to the wall and an armchair on the other side facing the couch. Against the wall next to the armchair stood a chest of drawers with a radio on top.

"After we unpack," I said facetiously, "we should sit down, have a beer, and decide what to do first."

Griffin turned on the radio, and sat on the armchair, Harris and Kelsey sat on the couch and Reggie and myself sat on the end of a couple of beds. We all opened a beer.

Kelsey said "I think we should get the tube to the center of London, find a pub that sells food, try some English beer and then get the train to Wembley."

We all agreed, and so the foundation for the day was laid.

We had no idea where we were in London, or even where the center of London was. The center of Edinburgh contained a magnificent castle high on a volcanic crag. We knew of no middle-ages castle high on a crag in London. We did know, that next to the River Thames (which flowed through the center of London) was the Tower of London. This, we made our target.

We went down to the reception area and I asked the woman standing in the reception hatch where we were.

"You're in 'ammersmiff dear."

"We're where?"

"'ammersmiff."

"She's trying to say Hammersmith," said Griffin.

"Now don't you try to come it with me lad, we know how to talk proper 'roun he-ah. Any more of that and you'll get a real clout roun' yer earole."

"Sorry," I said "can you tell us the easiest way to get to the Tower of London."

"Any more cheek and I'll show you the quickest way," she replied. "Down the road is 'ammersmiff station, take the green line and get off when it says Tower Hill."

We gave her our thanks and headed over to the station. Once outside we noticed the area had some good-looking pubs. Unfortunately, opening time was not quite upon us.

Chapter 10

The Auld Enemy – London

The trip to Tower Hill was very easy. The station had giant maps of the tube route painted on the walls and, inside the tube train there were more maps above the windows.

When we got out of the station at Tower Hill we were underwhelmed. The Tower of London paled in comparison to Edinburgh Castle, the Tower Bridge couldn't hold a candle to the Forth bridge and the River Thames was a rivulet compared to the mighty Firth of Forth.

But the most alarming thing, there was neither a Scotsman nor a pub in sight.

"Why in God's name did William Wallace and Bonnie Prince Charlie bring two armies south of the border with the aim of conquering this place?" said Reggie.

Kelsey answered "Well, you can see why the English kept invading Scotland. With such a beautiful spot just north of the border I would try to get out of here too."

"The Scottish armies got as far as the city of York, only 200 miles from here, and sent the whole of England into a tizzy" editorialized Harris. "The English had no soldiers between them and London and were terrified by these warriors from the north. They started to abandon London, but by that time, the rank-and-file Scots were homesick and realized this country just wasn't worth it. They said to their leaders "we've had enough," turned around and started marching home. Their Prince, lairds and chiefs could do nothing but follow them."

"How can you fight a war if the soldiers decide they don't like it and start going home?" said Reggie indignantly. "You might as well not bother in the first place."

"That's all well and good, but we still have to find a pub." I said. "It looks more promising if we start moving away from the river and into that populated area up the hill."

We walked about a half-mile then we saw some pubs with a group of Scots standing on the sidewalk drinking pints of beer.

We greeted them warmly and they said "Awa' in lads and try the beer. As usual, the bastard's are way over charging us for it, but tonight we'll get our own back!"

Not sure what they meant about getting our own back tonight we entered the pub. It contained only Scots. We set up in a corner of the bar and ordered beer and hot pies from a surly barkeep. For the next couple of hours, as the crowd sang every patriotic song they knew, we pleasantly imbibed in pints of best British ale washed down with pints of best British lager.

After a while shouts of "time to go" emanated from the patrons. The crowd rose, downed their drinks, and headed for the door.

"Where are you going?" we asked one of the departing Scots.

"To get the train to Wembley" he replied.

"Might as well follow them" said Harris.

We exited the pub and tagged along behind the group of drinkers. It must've been some kind of main thoroughfare because more Scots kept joining us from side streets. Soon we had a major procession walking down the road, flags waving and people singing. They stretched from side walk to side walk and gave not a single care for the traffic that formerly had right of way.

The procession entered the station. Whoever was in charge of the Wembley line was well prepared. A train was scheduled to leave for Wembley Stadium every few minutes, so we had no trouble climbing aboard one. The train was a commuter which traveled above ground. Unlike the

Tube, whose seating traveled along the wall and faced inward this train had more traditional seating which faced forward and backwards. There were also some regular London commuters sitting in the carriage we were in.

Griffin, inspired by the conversation we had with the lady in the reception hatch at our boarding house and fueled by a combination of Scottish and English beer decided to make the time we had with the Londoners into an elocution lesson.

There were no seats available so we were standing in the center aisle. Griffin moved down to the front of the carriage and faced the local commuters.

He opened with "How come you people in London cannot say the letter Haytch. If you completely dislike someone you don't say you ate them. People will think you're a cannibal. You have to get that Haytch on the beginning of the word. So after me. Let's all say it - Haytch - Haytch."

This elicited absolutely no response from his class apart from a slight concern that this drunken Scotsman would suddenly start wielding his broadsword.

"Okay, let's go to an easier example. This morning we checked into a boarding house in HHHHHammersmith. So, say after me *'this morning we checked into a boarding house in HHHHHammersmith'*." Nothing.

"You're going to have to end your lesson, we're almost there," said Harris.

A look of relief came over Griffin's class. But undaunted he carried on.

"All right, I've got one I know you can do. The word Hammersmith does not end with FF. It ends with a TH. Now, this is even easier, as all you have to do is put your tongue between your top and bottom front teeth try to say the letter ess."

He gave an example of doing this, but his disinterested class had returned to looking out the window or reading their magazines and newspapers.

The train was pulling up at Wembley Stadium station and Griffin said "Thank you for your time, here endeff the lesson."

All the Scots in the carriage gave him a big cheer.

Chapter 11

The Auld Enemy – The Game

We disembarked the train, exited the station and like thousands of others started the walk up the long gently sloping road towards the stadium. It was a bright sunny day and we could see shimmering in the sun, the fabled white towers which denoted the main entrance to the stadium.

Two solid dark lines of London police, affectionately known as Bobbies, stood on both sides of the road stretching all the way to the stadium. We had seen English Bobbies countless times on television wearing their unique peaked helmets, but it still seemed incongruous to see it in real life. We walked with the crowd up the road and after we had gone about half the distance to the stadium we came upon an unusual site.

As a preface to this, I have to tell you of a TV show that had been running for over 20 years on the BBC called Dixon of Dock Green. This was a rather mundane serial about a local London Bobby whose local beat (which he walks) is the fictitious Dock

Green area. He dispenses wisdom, justice and fair play in a down home manner to the residents. Throughout its life it had been an immensely popular, low key, crime drama.

The unusual site we had come across were three inebriated Scotsmen facing the police line and they had positioned themselves about one foot in front of the line. They were dancing a jig and singing to the tune of Camptown Races:

Who's that there with the black hat on,

Dixon Dixon

Who's that there with the black hat on,

Dixon of Dock Green,

On the beat all day,

On the wife all night,

Who's that there with the black hat on,

Dixon of Dock Green.

The police stood there, like Guardsmen in front of Buckingham Palace, demonstrating complete oblivion to what was going on right in front of them. If this had happened at a major event in Scotland the three merry makers would have disappeared, faster than a politician's promise. Their reappearance would be on Monday morning in front of a Magistrate, most likely charged with assaulting policemen by throwing themselves to the ground and repeatedly beating their heads against the policemen's feet.

We had to give due respect to the patience shown by the thin blue line.

Finally, we reached the stadium and made our way to our entrance gate. It was close to kickoff time and we did not want to miss the beginning. Outside the stadium stood thousands of Scotland supporters who had come south with the futile hope of obtaining tickets. We cleared the turnstile and made our way down the tunnel to our spot in the stadium. At that point in time, Wembley Stadium consisted of seventy-five percent terracing. Terracing were very wide steps that made it all the way to the top of the stadium. This is where you stood to watch the game. The other portion of the stadium had seats and curiously it was called the stand.

When we entered the stadium, the site was breathtaking. The stadium was bright white, the football pitch was dark green and in perfect condition, the sky was a brilliant blue.

But there was one more site that was truly awesome. The Tartan Army had arrived in full force and occupied one half of the stadium. For a stadium that held 82,000 people, the Scots had swept down from the north, at least 40,000 strong and they were in full throat. It was almost a medieval sight with thousands of banners and flags being held high and the majority of the Scots in some form of traditional dress. The only thing missing were tents and the pall of smoke from hundreds of campfires.

The singing and roaring continued all the way to the end of the game even though Scotland lost three goals to one. The result seemed, in the opinion of all the Scots present, the fault of the referee.

Chapter 12

The Auld Enemy - Aftermath

When the tartan Army began to exit the stadium, they were still in excellent spirits. We had our suspicions about what was fueling this level of euphoria. They seemed to know where they were going, and with our being neophytes to this part of the country we fell in to step with the bulk of the Army. It did not take long for us to get a very good clue as to where we were headed. Almost simultaneously, 20,000 fellow travelers on this road burst into song while clapping their hands or waving their flags.

Once again to the tune of Camptown races:

Piccadilly here we come,

Doodah Doodah,

etc.

I was sure that everyone between here and Piccadilly could hear this. I was also sure there would be much relief in areas of London not called Piccadilly.

The throng arrived at a Tube station and started to board trains. We looked at the map on the wall and saw we had one change which would get us to Piccadilly. It was a noisy, but uneventful journey and after a successful change of trains we disembarked at Piccadilly Circus station.

The station must have been deeply underground because it required two very long escalators to get to street level. The authorities realizing who were coming had, for safety reasons, shut down the escalators. This meant a long climb up the stationary escalators. But once again the Army had a plan to make the ascent enjoyable.

With uncanny coordination they began to jump from step to step. On Piccadilly Circus people heard a regular thrump, thrump, thrump drifting up from the bowels of the station. As it got louder they probably wondered for an instant if an ancient beast had woken and was about to lay waste to the center of London, until they remembered the Scots were here.

Newton's third law of motion (every action has an equal and opposite reaction) kicked in. Each jump pushed the escalators in; the reaction of the escalators was to push back out. This started a wave motion which became very pronounced and a little scary. Police and railroad officials were standing at the top and bottom of the escalators screaming at the Scots to stop jumping. They were completely ignored. To prevent catastrophic damage to the escalators, the police put a cordon at the bottom and rationed how many people could go at one time. This seemed to work, but it resulted in the platforms filling up beyond capacity. Trains were held outside the station until there was room enough for its passengers to disembark.

We finally emerged onto Piccadilly Circus, an area in central London similar to Times Square in New York. It is a wide circle with major roads and avenues feeding into it. There are buildings covered with large neon signs and it features, close to the center, the Shaftesbury Memorial. Atop the memorial is the statue of Eros, the God of love and desire.

The roads running into it contain famous stores, theaters, bars and restaurants. It is also next to ritzy areas such as Mayfair and very close to Buckingham palace.

The objective our group and the majority of the Scots who had headed for Piccadilly Circus was an adjoining district known as Soho.

Soho, is an area of very narrow serpentine streets. It contains pubs, restaurants, sex shops, strip clubs, peep shows, and hookers. We had never been to a strip club, so we had made this a top priority. We entered the labyrinth and were awed by the plethora of bright lights, neon signs and shop fronts full of marital aids. The hustle and bustle was intense. All around us were signs advertising the best strip clubs since Sodom and Gomorrah.

We selected one that had an entrance like a small cinema, the difference being you don't see so much neon and glitter outside a movie theater. At the front was a guy sitting in a booth collecting entrance fees. He was desperately trying to tell a bunch of Scots to furl their flags and lower their banners and posters before going in. The Scots on the other hand were more concerned about whether drinks were served in the theater.

After they went in we went up to the booth to pay for entry. Directly behind us was another group of Scots who had the clear intention of following us in. I had been warned before coming south to be careful about these strip clubs.

I said to the man in the booth. "After we pay you, there isn't going to be another man standing at the stage doorway who wants to charge us again, is there?"

The group behind us heard the question and one of them shouted at the booth man. "You better nae try and charge us twice or we're coming right back here and we'll take oor refund."

We entered the club closely followed by our new found friends. As we got to a second door, a man came from the side with his hand held up, obviously wanting to stop us. The man in the booth shouted down the hallway. "Fer Christ's sake, just let them through!"

We entered and were surprised to find a miniature theater, tiered seating, holding probably sixty people and a stage with closed curtains. It contained only Scots and the atmosphere was similar to Wembley. They had paid no heed to the man at the front desk and were waving their banners and flags while arguing with a man standing in front of the stage.

"Where do we buy the drinks." Was the predominant question.

"I keep telling you, we're not licensed to sell alcohol," he said.

"Yer just a wee sap. Luckily we brought our own."

"How many times do I have to tell you, you can't drink alcohol in here."

"Well, you just come up here and take it aff us ye wee wanker."

"If you start drinking there will be no show."

"If there's no show there'll be no theater!"

The man from the hallway came in and spoke quietly to the man in front of the stage. They both exited stage left. Music started up on some scratchy speakers and behind the curtain you could hear the clumping of someone coming down a stairway.

The curtain opened to reveal a woman wearing a tam, white blouse, tartan miniskirt and plaid knee length stockings. The crowd went wild, everyone standing whooping and hooching. She waved to the crowd and started doing the worst rendition of a highland fling I had ever seen. The jig sent the crowd into a frenzy. Cries such as "Marry me; I've a wee croft fur ye; Toss my caber; Wanna see my sporran;" came from all over the room.

I wondered how she was going to strip while doing a jig.

She was trying to time the jig to some stripper music and the two just didn't sync up. Nonetheless, spurred on by the massive enthusiasm she began to unbutton her blouse while her legs kept in time to the rhythmic clapping that had started. She got the blouse buttons undone and was able to discard it to a thunderous roar, she then started on the buckles of her mini kilt. This seemed easier than the blouse and it quickly hit the stage. The perspiration on her brow was now very obvious. Foot stamping had joined the hand clapping making the noise deafening, this seemed to give her a second wind. Beer and whisky was being passed up and down the rows fueling the fervor of the audience. Based on the noise, they must be lining up 30 deep outside trying to get into this show. She now turned her back to the audience and unclipped her bra, the noise subsided slightly as the anticipation rose. She jigged back to face the audience with her arms folded across her breasts.

Now the foot stamping and handclapping was joined by a chant of "do it, do it, do it!"

After teasing us for a few seconds she threw her arms in the air. The roar almost blew the roof off the theater. She did a twirl and then flung her tam into the audience, this was immediately followed by about 40 tams flying onto the stage. With an ecstatic smile on her face she did a graceful bow and the curtains closed.

An extended period of handclapping and congratulatory shouting followed. After a little bit, it was realized that there would not be an encore, so the audience started climbing onto the stage to collect their tams. This brought management back into the theater, but by this time, they realized anything they said was just futile. They let the tam collection go uncontested. We made our way to the front entrance and exited the theater. Outside in the street was a huge crowd waiting to get in.

"What's going on in there?" was the major question. "The noise coming out of that theater was deafening, even out here in the street."

"Wait until you boys get in, it's brilliant. There's a wee lassie on the stage who's the greatest dancer we've ever seen."

"Are they selling beer and whisky?"

"No, but they don't mind if you bring your own."

We made our way back into the Soho labyrinth and by pure accident ended up on Great Windmill Street, a narrow one-way street wide enough to accommodate only one vehicle and home of what was during World War II an internationally famous institution known as the Windmill Theater.

Running for about half a mile it connects Shaftesbury Avenue with Brewer Street. Midway between these streets it is bisected by Ham Yard on one side and another narrow street called Archer Street on the other. This intersection contained the Windmill Theatre on one corner, two pubs diagonally across from each other and what looked like a boxing gym on the fourth corner. It also contained hundreds of Scotsmen standing in the intersection and overflowing into all roads leading to the intersection. They were drinking pints of beer and other and all types of sundry drinks. It looked like an ideal spot for us to continue our refreshment purchases.

We made our way into one of the pubs and immediately saw why there was such a crowd outside. Inside was packed and they were five deep at the bar ordering drinks. The bar appeared to have about 10 barmen, one every 3 feet, working as hard and as fast as I have ever seen anybody pouring drinks.

"Everybody having a pint?" I asked (as if I had to). After the assenting nods I said "I'll go to the bar and if you stick close I'll pass them back to you."

I shoved my way to the bar and ordered the pints. As they were pulled I passed them back to the others. When complete we bulldozed our way back into the street. Once there, I understood what the Scot meant earlier that day when he said we would get them back this evening for over charging. Outside, once a patron had finished his drink he smashed the glass on the ground and made his way back into the pub for another. This was going on all around us, so not to be outdone, once we finished our pints we smashed the glasses on the ground and headed back in for another round.

Even though it was a very narrow one-way street filled with Scottish drunks, the occasional car still eased its way through the crowd. One such vehicle was a Mini Cooper with four, as they were referred to then, Dolly birds in it. As they eased their way through the horde they were waving and blowing kisses. This got the throngs attention. They closed in all around and brought the car to a halt. Unable to move, the waving and blowing of kisses from the girls came to a hesitant halt. All the waving and blowing of kisses was now coming from outside the car.

I was fairly close to the action and I started shouting "turn it around, turn it around."

This struck those gathered around the car as a good idea. The closest ones reached down onto the underside of the car and hefted it into the air. Then, like a rugby scrum performing a wheel, they shuffled right until the car was facing the way it came. The car was gently placed back on the ground and the scrum stepped back to admire their handiwork. The car, now pointing the wrong way on a one-way street, offered no alternative to the driver other than to put it in reverse and start slowly backing up all the way to the main intersection. If looks could kill, there would have been a slaughter on Great Windmill Street.

I had separated from the rest of our group and was standing with my beer at the edge of the crowd next to Archer Street. There was a fairly attractive woman standing there looking at the crowd. Long brown hair, spiky high heels, miniskirt and a low-cut top.

"Hello" I said "did you come to take a look at what the Scots do on a Saturday night."

"It looks like a lot of fun" she said. "I wish it was like this down here every Saturday night, it's usually very quiet."

"You're welcome to join in, later on we will be going back to our hotel and will probably party for the rest of the night. If you want, you can come back with us."

"Where's your hotel?"

"Hammersmith."

"Who the fuck gets a hotel in Hammersmith!"

"It's a great place, pubs all around, and our room is not only huge, it has two couches and five beds. In the morning I can sneak you onto our coach and smuggle you into Scotland."

"You want me to spend the night with you in Hammersmith and then get on a bus and go to Scotland. What the hell do you think I am?!?"

"I thought you were a party girl looking for a good time."

"Looking for a good time!" she spluttered. "Are all you Scots quite insane?"

"I take it that's a no?"

"You can take it any way you want but I'll tell you what I'm going to do. My apartment is just down the road, and my boyfriend is in there waiting for me. I'm going to tell him to come down to this corner and sort out you bunch of drunks."

With that, she spun on her heels and went stomping off down the road.

I thought, 'she's going to go up to her apartment and tell her boyfriend to go down to the corner and launch an assault against several hundred drunken Scotsmen. That's going to be a short conversation.'

I forced my way back into the crowd and crunched across the broken glass until I saw Griffin having a conversation with a man standing at the entrance to the boxing gym.

Griffin looked at me and said to the man "Here's the guy I was telling you about, the Lothian and Borders Welterweight Boxing Champion."

"Nice to meet you," said the man. "Would you like to come up and spar a few rounds?"

"Normally I would, but this weekend is dedicated to football and beer, plus I don't want to hurt anybody."

Our conversation was interrupted by a loud blast on a horn. We turned around to see a guy driving a shiny new Jaguar forcing his way through the crowd. The crowd was not taking kindly to his honking and revving of the engine. The driver seemed to finally lose patience and started to accelerate through the crowd causing people to leap for their lives. He broke through leaving people sprawled everywhere and with the squeal of tire spin started to pull away.

The sky suddenly filled with flying beer glasses arcing towards the car. There was no way the Jag was going to outrun this aerial assault. The glasses started crashing on the hood, roof and trunk of the car. The back window was completely smashed by a couple of well-placed throws.

The car screeched to a halt and the driver's door started to open. At that point a second wave of glasses took to the air. I assumed that these were from the Scots who wanted to finish their drinks before throwing their glass. The second wave was equally as deadly and this time managed to shatter the front windshield and take off a mirror.

Mr. Road Rage had had enough. The front door slammed shut and the Jag accelerated away and fishtailed as it rounded the corner onto the main street.

A cheer of victory went up and shouts of "Let's see if he comes around again for a second go."

We went back into the pub for more beer but were told that we had to bring back our used glasses as they seemed to have run out. With that bit of bad news we decided to head down to Piccadilly Circus to see what was happening.

When we got to Piccadilly we were greeted by an almost surreal scene. The sidewalk all the way around the Circus was seven or eight people deep. All of them Scots. They were standing there silently staring at the three rings of policemen surrounding the statue of Eros. Whether some kind of coordinated charge had been planned I did not know, but the ring of police standing in the center did not look very happy. I think they would have preferred the raucous singing, dancing, and drinking that they were used to seeing.

We decided to head back to Hammersmith. We were all very inebriated and for some reason I decided that the entrance to the tube station was over by the statue of Eros.

"Are you sure?" said Harris.

"That's the way we came in" I said. "Follow me and we'll go and get the train."

I stepped off the curb and headed towards the center of the circle with the rest of the group in line behind me. The police standing in the center looked at me rather curiously as I approached.

When I reached them I said "Excuse me can I get through?"

"What do you mean you want to get through?"

"Me and my friends want to go down to the tube station."

"What friends?"

I turned around and no one was behind me, I looked back, my posse was still on the sidewalk smiling at me.

I turned back to the police officer and said "sorry I must've made a mistake."

I then headed back towards the sidewalk. About halfway there cheering and clapping started from the crowd who had enjoyed the lone walker. I did not dare to acknowledge their appreciation as I felt the police may take this the wrong way.

Once I was safely back among the crowd I asked my cohorts "Why the hell did you let me walk out there on my own?"

"We were curious to see if you would get arrested," said Kelsey. "Anyway the tube station is right there."

He pointed towards the tube station entrance about 20 feet from where we stood.

We caught the tube and had an uneventful ride back to Hammersmith. We headed towards our boarding house and as we got close we found a pub that was really rocking. Inside were many of our fellow coach travelers having a high old-time. The jukebox was blaring, tables had been pushed to one side to make a temporary dance floor and drinks were flowing like water. What made things even better was the place was chockablock with women.

We got our drinks and started chatting to a few of the girls. To our joy they couldn't be friendlier. Pretty soon we were dancing, hugging, buying drinks, kissing and having a grand time.

"Why do you all have to go back to Scotland tomorrow?" my new girlfriend asked, her face all pouty.

"Because our country needs us" I replied. I had learned my lesson, so I did not ask her to come back with us on the bus.

The revelries continued but inevitably came the cry of "time gentlemen please" from the landlord. I think he was as disappointed as we were that it was closing time due to the cracking business he was doing.

"No problem," I said to my gathered flock "it's back to our place!"

We left the pub with the girls and headed up the road to our boarding house; a short journey accompanied with a lot of noise, swaying and sashaying. No one really knew who was holding who up.

Arriving at our room we set the lights low cranked up the radio and pulled out our reserve stockpile of beer. Soon everything was going just like it was in the pub, dancing, kissing and fondling.

I was sitting on the end of my bed facing the fireplace and sofas with my new fiancée on my knee. Kelsey was sitting on the sofa, his girlfriend stretched out with her head in his lap. She was dressed in a tank top and bright pink satin hotpants.

I turned to Griffin who was laying back on his bed with his girlfriend. "Griffin, do you notice anything unusual about Kelsey's girl?"

Griffin edged himself up onto his elbows, took a look and said "do you mean apart from the fact she seems to have either soiled her hotpants or spilled a drink on them?"

"I saw that, but that's not what I meant. If you look closely her left leg appears to be a prosthetic."

He looked again, recognition dawning on his face "My God! Kelsey has managed to pick up the only one-legged hooker in London."

Chapter 13

The Auld Enemy – Homeward

Bound

The rest of the night went by in a drunken blur. None of us could ever recollect what went on. We were woken to a loud banging of a gong outside in the hallway. This was the signal that the coach was here and everyone should climb aboard. We struggled from our beds, feeling decidedly under the weather, and gazed at the devastation of our room.

"Holy crap!" said Reggie "just look at this!"

"Never mind." I said "If anyone says anything we can just deny it." I then whispered "We'll tell them that the room was perfect when we left and those girls we left in there must have trashed it."

We made our way downstairs and met up with the rest of the passengers who looked in an even sorrier state than we were. On the bus there was complete silence as everyone settled back for the long journey. I looked out the coach window. Across the road at a bus stop was a man standing in top hat, white tie and tails holding a posy of flowers. A bit unusual for a bus stop at 8 o'clock in the morning I thought, but what the hell, this is London.

The coach started up and pulled away from our boarding house. Soon we had cleared the northern suburbs of London and were on the main highway back to Scotland.

As I drifted towards sleep, I thought of our previous conversation about Scottish armies that had fought and marched all the way down here then decided it's not worth it, we're going home. It reminded me of a verse from a Byron poem.

For the sword outwears its sheath,

And the soul wears out the breast,

And the heart must pause to breathe,

And love itself have rest.

Chapter 14

Camping

I had recently bought a two-man pup tent. My friend Griffin Tompkinson thought, for our summer holidays, it would be a good idea to go on a camping trip. We kicked around a few areas and finally decided to go to Newquay, a seaside town in Cornwall.

This would be as far a journey as we could make and still remain on the main island of the United Kingdom. Cornwall was, and still is, referred to as the English Riviera. Situated in South West England the sun, surf, plenty of campgrounds and lots of girls made it an ideal destination for us.

We accumulated the rest of the gear needed for camping and, since we hadn't used any of the stuff, thought it would be a good idea to give it a trial run. We selected a local spot, loaded the gear in Griffin's car and in the evening set off for the campsite. It was only a 15-minute drive so on the way we stopped at one of our favorite watering holes. By the time we got back in the car it was quite dark.

We drove to our overnight stay area, unloaded the car, and using lanterns pitched our tent. Being mildly anesthetized from our stop at the pub, we got into our sleeping bags and were soon sound asleep.

We were abruptly awakened early next morning by the most God awful roar coming from directly above us. We flipped open the tent flap and there in front of us was a commercial airliner about to crash. It did not crash, instead it made a perfect landing on a runway. We scrambled out of the tent and looking around realized we were nowhere close to our desired campsite.

Commercial airports, at the end of the runway, have rows of approach lights which are mounted on the top of poles. Furthest away from the runway are the tallest poles and they diminish in size as they get closer. This gives landing aircraft a glide path. We were camped in the midst of one of these light forests.

It was obviously Edinburgh Turnhouse airport. Noise restrictions prevent takeoffs and landings during certain night hours. We had stumbled in when the lights were switched off. How we managed to avoid walking into one of the poles as we made camp was astounding.

In those days' security at airports was not nearly as strict as it is now. However, we did know camping on the end of a runway at an international airport was probably forbidden. We grabbed everything and just threw it in the car. We jumped in, and as we peeled out, another jetliner came roaring over us.

We made a clean getaway. Later, in another pub, we reflected on the incident and agreed, if a pilot had indeed reported sighting us, no one would believe anyone would be stupid enough to camp there.

Undaunted by this first hitch, we continued with our preparations for the trip to Cornwall.

The big day came and we set off reasonably early – at least for us – on a Saturday morning. The journey was approximately 550 miles, most of it motorway, so we estimated our travel time at nine hours. We made great time on the motorway, very rarely being passed by another vehicle; obviously the driver of any vehicle that did pass us was a complete nutcase.

Radio at that time in the UK, I believe, was all AM. It was great reception but every time we drove under an overpass the radio would completely fade out for a few seconds. We amused ourselves for quite a while by singing along with radio and when we hit an underpass we would fade our voices down to nothing for a few seconds and then resume.

The trouble started when we exited the motorway and began our journey, on regular highways, through the West country. As we approached the town of Bridgwater we ran into a massive backup. It took us several hours to get into Bridgwater and by then it was late evening. We decided to stop at a pub, get something to eat and some liquid refreshment, then find a spot nearby to camp overnight.

We parked at a likely looking pub in the center of town. When we walked inside we realized we'd hit the jackpot. The place was jumping; all people our age. It even had two or three bouncers so obviously it was going to get even livelier.

Bridgwater lies in the county of Somerset. Somerset is famous for a locally brewed hard cider called Scrumpy. It is made primarily from apples but there are a lot of myths about how the local farmers brew it. Some say they use rotten apples to give it more potency; others say they throw a dead calf in the vat and when it's been totally dissolved the Scrumpy is ready. No matter what, Scrumpy is a very intoxicating drink, enjoyable but somewhat flat and murky.

You cannot get Scrumpy in Scotland. A little strange for a country that boasts the wonderfulness of Haggis. We were very keen to try it and ordered a couple of pints. As the evening wore on we were feeling no pain and getting on well with the locals. English law was a little laxer than Scotland and closing time was 11 o'clock. At this bewitching hour, the traditional call of "time gentlemen please" began to be called by the bartenders. We were standing at the bar with our Scrumpy's (not the ones we started off with) and the barman came over to take them away from us.

In unison we said "Not a F'ng chance!"

"Give me the drinks or I'll call the bouncers."

"You call them bouncers, where we come from bouncers stand on mountains and throw hills at each other."

At that point the manager, having noticed the developing fracas came down the bar and said "You two jocks, give us the glasses!"

"Just as soon as they are empty" replied Griffin.

"Right!" said the manager and went striding down the bar to the exit door.

We finished our drinks and joined the throng who were leaving. When we got to the door, the manager pointed at us and said to the bouncers, "Don't let them out."

The bouncers and the manager screened us off from the door as the remaining revelers left. A barman then closed the door. We both knew that there was going to be some trouble. Griffin, staring at the manager, said "There's ten more of us outside, if we don't go out, they're going to come in."

The manager paused for a couple of seconds and turned around to the barman at the door and said "let them out."

His bluff had worked. Thank goodness for all the trouble the Scots cause when they go down to Wembley. The news had obviously reached Bridgwater.

We got back in the car and headed in the direction of Newquay. The roads were busy, but once we got out of Bridgwater the traffic died down to almost nothing.

"I'll keep my eye open for a spot where we can camp for the night" I said.

Shortly, we were driving down a two lane road and I spotted to our right that the grass had been cut and there were no bushes or trees. It was a perfect spot for us to overnight. Griffin pulled onto the grass and we made camp. The Scrumpy had really taken its toll, and in conjunction with the long drive we were really looking forward to our sleeping bags.

The following morning we were lying in the tent feeling the ill effects of the Scrumpy.

"From the sound of things, traffic has really picked up on the road" said Griffin.

I replied "I hope we don't get into another traffic jam like yesterday, let me take a look." I opened the flap, stepped out and groaned "Oh no, not again."

From the tent came "Is there something wrong?"

"Come out here and take a look."

Griffin crawled out of the tent and took a look at what I was staring at. We had camped in the median of a four-lane highway. Fortunately, it was Sunday morning and the traffic was fairly light. However, all the occupants of every car that drove by on either side were staring at us. Some cars honked their horns.

"I don't think we should stay to cook breakfast."

A couple of hours later we had reached Newquay. We could have made it sooner but we had to stop frequently to throw up.

On the outskirts of the town we found a fairly large commercial campsite called 'Elves Mines'. Caravans were lined up close to the front gate next to the rental office and general store. The tenting community, all in neat rows, was spread out in the rear. The tent pitches were of various sizes depending on the size of the tent. Since we had only a two-man pup tent and a small car (Hillman Imp) we were directed to the row with the smallest pitches; these came at a very reasonable price. The campground had toiletry and bathing facilities and even a laundry. Additionally, there were no airport runways or four-lane highways running through it. Quite a unique experience for us.

It was a very enjoyable holiday and we met lots of nice people. There was only one incident – and I will refer to it as minor – during our stay.

We met a couple of girls, Rita and Michelle, who were in a tent nearby. The four of us had gone to the beach and various pubs in the town several times. Late evenings we would hang out near our tents, usually with a fellow group of happy campers. After a few days we had paired off, Rita and I having a holiday romance and likewise with Griffin and Michelle.

One evening Griffin and I were in a very large pub in Newquay. It had a billiards room, a stage, a dance floor, chairs and tables and a very long bar. We were standing in the billiards room because people were packed into all the other areas. A clear glass partition with a door set in the center of it separated the billiards room from the rest of the pub.

As we were studying the throng we wondered why the place was so busy. About then the door at the end of the billiards room opened. Through it came two bouncers followed by a Glam band, in full Glam gear, carrying their guitars. They exited the billiards room through the door in the partition and headed up to the stage. We recognized them as 'Sweet'; well known for their top 20 hit 'Little Willy'. They were just hitting their peak so we were very surprised to see them playing in this establishment. Our instincts told us, if we hung around in the billiards room till the band was finished, there would be a lot a very excited single young ladies milling around. Things could work out well.

We didn't have to wait long. We started talking to a couple of girls who were watching the band through the glass partition that separated the billiards room from the dance floor. To our amazement they were also from our campground and said they'd noticed us.

Sweet finished playing around 10 o'clock. The girls suggested we get some beer and meet up at their tent in "Elves Mines." This was agreeable to us and we all headed back.

The girls, who we now knew as Sheila and Rosie, had a tent a few rows up from ours. Compared to our tent, it was a mansion. We sat under their covered front porch and became progressively more amorous with each other. The camp had a 12 o'clock curfew. After this time groups could not sit outside their tents talking or singing, have outside lights on, or use camp stoves. When the curfew fell Griffin and Sheila headed down to our tent and I went into Rosie's casa de mala reputacion.

The next day we had plans to go to a sauna with Rita and Michelle. This was a spa with self-contained private saunas; each had a plunge pool of chilled water directly outside. The technique was to sit in the sauna until you were completely covered in sweat - and as hot as you could stand - then run outside and jump in the pool. You keep repeating this process until your time is up. Bathing suits are required.

Griffin and I were at our tent readying ourselves when Griffin said, "What's that on your back?"

"What do you mean, what's that on my back?"

"It looks like a giant R."

"Must've been Rosie's idea of a joke, I'll go to the showers and wash it off."

"You're not washing that off."

"You think it's been done in indelible ink?"

"More like indelible hickeys."

"Is it very noticeable?"

"Only if someone can see you."

I thought for a few moments and then said "There's really no way of getting out of the sauna trip. I'd say I was under the weather but I'm not lying in a little tent all day."

"You'll be wearing a shirt most of the time, all you have to do in the sauna is keep your front pointed towards them."

"That means when we jump in the pool I'll have to be first out the door and running backwards. It's going to look a little strange."

Later that day as we were walking over to meet the girls I said to Griffin "I have an idea. My name begins with an R and Rita's does also. You can say that you did the R with a bicycle tire pump as a tribute to the two of us."

"Only if you do a G and M on my back and I want them done in script. I also want a rose between the two letters."

"Okay, okay, so you don't want to be involved, I'll go with the 'keeping my front to them' plan."

We met up with the girls and headed over to the spa, a fairly short drive. Once there we donned swimsuits in our respective changing rooms and headed for our sauna cabin.

As we were walking over Rita asked me "Are you going to wear a T-shirt in the sauna?"

"I'll take it off when we get there, it will take the chill off when we are done."

Our sauna was constructed of wooden staves and resembled a barrel lying on its side. I got to the door first so I could do a quick reconnaissance. On either side there were benches against the curved walls. The stove was against the wall at the far end. The spa called it a four-person sauna but it seemed cramped. I reckoned it was about six feet in diameter and about seven feet long with the stove taking up at least two feet of the length. Keeping my R undetected might prove more difficult than I thought.

Griffin, claiming that he knew how much water to splash on the stones atop the stove, went in first. Rita and Michelle followed him and sat on either bench. I went in and sat by the door next to Rita. These were pretty tight quarters and it was difficult for me to swivel my body as I took my T-shirt off. Having accomplished that, I sat in the curved corner trying to keep my torso at a 45° angle between Rita and Michelle. With the heat and the twisting, I was pretty damn uncomfortable. A new plan began to form in my head. I will have to be brazen.

"Rita, when we get out of the plunge pool I have something of a surprise for you."

"Looking forward to it" she said, with a slight look of bewilderment. Where could someone wearing only swim shorts be hiding a surprise?

We reached the point where we needed to cool down, I got up and backed out of the door. I held it open while facing everyone as they dashed out of the sauna and jumped into the plunge pool.

Griffin was last, as he passed me he whispered "This surprise better not have anything to do with me doing a tribute to you and Rita."

I jumped into the pool, the change in temperature almost stopped my heart but the absurdity of backing up the steps kept me in the water. I edged over to the steps and sat halfway up facing the others.

"Rita, remember I spoke to you about me getting a tattoo of an R for Rita."

"No?"

"You must, you said I shouldn't get anything so permanent."

"I remember nothing about that."

"Okay, but you must remember the couple we met on the beach by the surf shop the other day."

"Cindy and Paul, what about them?"

"Griffin and I met them yesterday afternoon when you and Michelle were shopping in town. We sat on the beach, drinking beer, getting some sun and just shooting the breeze. I mentioned that you were not keen on me getting an R tattoo."

"I still don't remember anything about a tattoo." She interrupted.

"Anyway, Cindy had an idea about a not so permanent R."

"And?"

I stood up and turned around.

There were a few moments of silence then Rita said "Paul let Cindy do that to you?"

"He certainly didn't do it, he thought it was a great laugh."

Griffin said "I'm getting cold, let's get back in the sauna."

We re-entered the sauna and sat at our previous positions.

Michelle said "It must have taken quite a while to create such a detailed R on your back?"

"Not really, I hardly felt a thing."

"Stand up and let me see it again" Said Rita.

I stood up in front of the door with my back towards Rita, head touching the roof and my knees slightly bent. Suddenly, there was this almighty sting across my back. This was followed by another then another. I spun around and there was Rita wielding one of the two sauna switches. About a foot long and made from multiple narrow pieces of silver birch they were shaped like the end of a witch's broom.

Designed to let a sauna user stimulate their muscles by gently whipping themselves, Rita was using it like she was beating a carpet.

After a few welts I was able to stop the assault by grabbing the business end of the switch.

Rita stood up, let go of the switch, and with a sardonic look uttered, "Oh yeah!" as she left.

Without a word, or a look sideways, Michelle followed directly behind.

"Nice job" said Griffin, "Did you create that master plan as you were sitting on the bench?"

"It's not the end of the world, let's go and find Rosie and Sheila. Since it's Rosie's fault I'll get her to rub some salve into my wounds."

Chapter 15

The Dunfermline Dreep

One evening there was great excitement at the Cramond Inn.

The inn lay at the bottom of a hill, next to where the river Almond joined the Firth of Forth. A road, called Glebe Street, ran up the hill for about half a mile and at the top intersected with a main road. Next to this junction was a bus stop where city buses ran every few minutes. There was a stonewall, about six feet high, that separated the road and the sidewalk from fields which gently sloped down towards the Firth of Forth.

Over the last year a large scale construction project had been taking place in those fields. Because of the campus style buildings that were being erected we had assumed it was something to do with the University of Edinburgh.

It was the falsity of this assumption that was causing the excitement that evening.

Indeed, a college campus was being built but it had nothing to do with the University of Edinburgh. The news had arrived that this was Dunfermline College, a woman's physical education school. Upon completion, hundreds of future gym teachers from all over the UK would be living there.

With the convenient adjacency of the Cramond Inn to the college it was almost certain that the pub would become a much busier place.

In the Autumn the college opened. Groups of students, led by guides walked down Glebe Street to the main esplanade. They were shown the rivers the beach the general store the Cramond Inn, both pub and restaurant, and the riverside walk that led up to the Cramond Brig.

Gradually, in the evenings, pockets of students began to trickle in to the Cramond Inn. People, including myself and my friends, were polite and helpful to these newcomers. After a while they became regulars and we, as long time regulars, grew friendly with them.

The college decided to help integrate its population with the local community and began to encourage the students to have social gatherings on Saturday nights. Any excuse could be used as a reason for these gatherings. It could be someone's birthday, an engagement, Robert Burns night, a high tide, a low tide, it was raining, it was windy, full moon, etc.

The venue for the socials was the college Recreation Center. The center would be set up with tables and chairs. A dance floor, complete with DJ (usually one of the students) was created and a heavily discounted cash bar served refreshments.

It was an attempt by the college to create a student union similar to the one run by their big brother, the University of Edinburgh.

My friends and I had become friendly with a wide number of students and I believe we were invited to every one of the socials. If we missed an invitation, we would go by the rec center on a Saturday night and see if anything was going on. If there was, we would go in, always to be welcomed.

Because of the liberal pouring of alcohol at these events I would arrive and leave by bus. I had to be mindful of the time due to the last bus leaving at 11:30 PM.

There was a night however, that I did miss the last bus.

It was a cracking evening with great conversation, lots of dancing and lashes of beer. I completely lost all sense of time and before I knew it, it was 1 AM. The lights came up to announce the end of the soirée.

"Well, I have a helluva walk in front of me, probably take over an hour. I hope it's not raining" I announced to all those sitting at my table.

"No problem RJ" said one of the girls at the table. "You can crash in our room tonight, the buses start running at 6 AM, just get out very early and no one will be any the wiser."

"Great, that will save me quite a hike."

They helped me sneak into their room and we cracked open some beer we had brought up from the rec hall.

The next morning, I was woken by someone shaking my shoulder and heard,

"RJ, RJ wake up, we've overslept. It's past 9 o'clock."

I rolled over, got to my feet, uncovered my hand from my eyes and began to cautiously open them. The harsh light of day was pouring in and the two girls were sitting on their beds looking at me.

"Well, I had better get going. Which is the way out?"

"You can't go walking down the hallway and out the front door. As the only man in the place you're bound to be noticed and all hell will break loose."

"All right, there must be an alternative, do you have a fire escape?"

"You can't go through the fire escape, as soon as you open the door the alarm will go off."

"Do you have any alternatives?"

"You'll have to go out the window."

"No problem. You should have mentioned that in the first place."

As I stepped towards the window I looked at the girls and said.

"That was a great night, I'll see you down at the pub."

I reached the window and looked out, then I looked down.

"You didn't mention we were on the second story."

"It's not too far of a drop, you can make it."

"If I jump out the window the law of gravity will make sure I make it. I just don't want to break both my legs in the process."

"You'll be fine, just do a dreep."

When I was a kid we would play a game called dreeping. It involved climbing a wall and hanging from the top, hands above your head holding on to the edge and dropping to the ground. This was called a dreep. The winner of the game was the kid who had the nerve to dreep from the highest height.

The girls wanted me to dreep from their window.

"Directly below there's a border that's been dug up to plant spring flowers" said one of the girls.

I looked down and saw a freshly dug border of soft earth about 3 feet wide running along the side of the building. About another 3 feet from the border was a paved path also running down the side of the building.

"Okay," I said. "I don't want you to get into trouble so I'll do it."

I opened the window, stuck my head out and took a scan of the area to make sure there was no one around. Quickly I clambered out, grabbed the edge of the sill and lowered my body down. The window was swiftly closed behind me so there was no going back.

As I hung there, gaining the final piece of courage to let myself go, I heard a strange noise. Squeak, squeak, squeak, squeak, squeak.

At that point a gardener came walking around the corner of the building pushing a wheelbarrow full of spring bulbs. He looked up at me and without breaking stride said,

"G'mornin."

"Good morning to you," I replied.

As if nothing unusual was going on, he carried on down the path towards the far end of the building.

'I had better drop' I thought and for some strange reason, to lessen the height of the drop, I pointed my feet straight down.

I let go.

The landing was not letter perfect. Because of the freshly dug soft earth, my pointed toes went straight in. My feet followed into the earth and took an angle towards the building. With the force I had hit the ground and the acute angle my feet were taking underneath me I had lost all control and no amount of arm windmilling could stop me from pitching backwards. My shoulders hit the ground first and then the back of my head went crack on the paved path.

I lay there for a couple of dazed seconds with stabs of pain shooting through my ankles and the blow to my head making me feel slightly nauseous. The thought, 'how could I explain this if anyone comes by' flashed through my mind. A feeling of potential intense embarrassment drove me to my feet.

Holding the back of my head and limping on both ankles I headed for the gate.

"Hey you!" came a loud shout from behind me.

I lowered my hand from the back of my head and turned to see two very officious, and magnificently toned, women standing about 20 yards from me.

"Yes you!" one called as they strode towards me.

Knowing flight was not an option I waited until they were directly in front of me.

"What are you doing on these grounds?"

Inspiration took over.

"Before the college was built on these fields I used them to tend a flock of sheep. I was waiting on a bus by the entrance and thought I would come in for one final reminiscence of my shepherding days."

My eyes were tearing up, not because of any emotion I felt towards my phantom flock, but as I stood there, severe pain was shooting through both my ankles. Their look softened and I think they started to feel a little sorry for me.

"You must miss those days," said one of the women "why don't you come on in and we'll give you a nice cup of tea."

I thought of the panic that would envelop both of the girls who had hosted me last night if they walked in to the refectory and saw me drinking tea with two prefects.

"I would love to do that," I replied "but I have to get to church, I'm giving a eulogy this morning."

"Okay," one said "but you are welcome back anytime."

"I will certainly do that."

And with these words we parted company.

Chapter 16

The Nun

I can honestly say in all the years I have been around I have never met a nun.

Chapter 17

The Americans -Part 1

Every year, for three weeks in August, Edinburgh hosts the world's largest arts festival. On stages, numbering into the hundreds, thousands of entertainers cater to all tastes by performing cabaret, music, comedy, spoken word, theater, dance, musicals, opera, children's shows and various other events. People attracted from all over the world pack the city.

In the very heart of Edinburgh, on one of the main thoroughfares, is a splendid building called the Assembly Rooms. Designed and built in the late 1700s it has over the years progressed from a meeting and socializing hall into a major venue for arts and social events. Due to its music hall, grand ballroom and rooms that can be used for private events it became the epicenter for the festival. During the festival the ballroom becomes a huge bar where hundreds gather every evening. It is called the Festival Club and requires you to purchase a membership for the duration of the festival.

Being economical, I did not purchase a membership, but I knew quite a few members and often attended as their guest.

One day I went to the Festival Club on my own on the chance that I would be able to slip in. As I purposely strode through the door one of the guards looked at me and said,

"Can I see your card sir?"

Without hesitation I reached into my inside pocket pulled out a flip card and with it slightly open flashed it at him as I went by. I put it back in my pocket and carried on without further incident.

Now, this was not a Festival Club membership card but my blood donor card. Before I entered I had it in the back of my mind, that should I be challenged, I would flash this card.

The beauty of the card is it is a hard sided, deep blue flip card with the gold logo of the Scottish Medical Association on the outside. Your name and blood type are on the inside. When seen quickly it seems very official. I now felt I could get into the club anytime I wanted.

A few days later I was wandering around the center of Edinburgh enjoying the sights, crowds and street acts. It got past 5 o'clock and I thought I'll find a pub and have a refreshment. I headed for Rose Street, a narrow single lane street that in the space of under a mile contains over 34 pubs. This street was famous for the 'Rose Street Pub Crawl'. You start at one end with the aim to enter every pub and drink a beer until you reached the other end. Many started, very few finished.

I was just approaching the junction with Rose Street when I passed a new establishment proudly calling itself 'Jackson's Wine Bar'. Wine bars were a new phenomenon in Edinburgh and I had never been in one. I thought I would give it a try.

I entered and was immediately in a world I had never been in before. Heretofore, I was used to dimly lit pubs with highly polished but worn bar tops, wooden stools, wooden tables, walls paneled in wood and an atmosphere laden with tobacco smoke. If the pub had windows they would be so heavily etched with designs you couldn't see through them. There may be a mirror behind the bar but the shelving and dozens of liquor bottles in front of it would make it impossible to see yourself. There would also be a nice Brass foot rest along the length of the bar and possibly a brass arm rest as well.

I stood just inside the entrance to the wine bar and thought I had entered the fourth dimension. The door I had just come through was floor to ceiling glass. The walls on either side of the door were also floor-to-ceiling glass. To keep this theme going, the left-hand wall consisted only of floor-to-ceiling glass. In the ceiling shone rows of bright lights.

To my right was a bar with a spotless mirrored back and a row of lights above to emphasize the wine bottles displayed behind the bar. The bar itself had a Formica top and the front of the bar from the top to the floor, and all along the length, was one-inch square, mirrored tiles. A few, elbow high, glass topped tables with no stools stood in the center of the floor. Rounded at the ends, they were about five feet long and a couple of feet wide. Mirrored tiles were also wrapped around them. In front of the glass wall were some glass topped tables with chrome legs. These you could sit at using clear plastic chairs with chrome legs. In front of the bar were some stools with, you guessed it, chrome legs and see-through plastic seats. The difference here was the seats were shaped like a pair of buttocks.

The place was fairly busy so I made my way to a buttock stool on the corner of the bar and sat down.

The barman came over and looked at me a little loftily.

To make conversation I said "You don't often see solid Formica tops in bars, do you?"

"No sir, this is a Florentine solid marble top. What can I get you?"

"How about a pair of sunglasses and a pint of lager."

"I assume you're joking about the sunglasses, and we don't sell draft beer."

"That's okay, I'll just have a bottle of lager."

"Sir, as you entered the premises did you notice above the door it said 'Jackson's Wine Bar'."

"I did, but I notice on the tables you have nuts and crackers, and on the bar you also have olives."

"We are still a wine bar."

"All right, what kind of spirits do you have?"

"Sir, I would urge you to step outside and read the sign above the door."

"I get it, you're a wine bar catering to the nuts and olives crowd. Okay, I'll have a glass of Mateus Rose."

"If you're after a nice Mateus I would recommend a Chinese restaurant."

"Then how about a glass of Blue Nun."

"I'm sorry sir, we don't stock that."

"I thought for a moment, then exhausted my knowledge of wines by asking him "do you have Chianti, you know the one that comes in the squat bottle inside a basket?"

"Ah, sir is referring to the Ruffino. Unfortunately, we have no red and white checkered tablecloths or candles so we do not stock it."

I was beginning to feel I was in the Monty Python cheese shop skit; it just needed a man in the corner playing a balalaika.

A couple of customers had approached the bar and were waiting for the barman and I to conclude our business. The barman was giving anxious sideways glances to the unserved patrons.

Realizing this was not a 'Chuck you out' type of establishment, and determined to have a glass of wine, irrespective of this polyester prat's condescending attitude, I pressed on.

"I would like something pink and fizzy, what would you recommend?"

"I have a very nice rouge from Sancerre, a vineyard located in the Loire valley or perhaps sir would prefer a Miraval - a wine produced in Provence, a region in the south of France. I think you would enjoy either."

"Thanks for the geography lesson, could I see one of the bottles?"

"Certainly."

He opened the glass cooler behind the bar and pulled out a bottle. Handing it to me he said, "this is one of our finest pink and fizzy wines."

I looked at the bottle and saw the vintage was 1973. "Haven't you got anything a bit newer?"

"That is a wonderful year."

"How much is it?"

He told me the price and I responded with "I don't want to treat the whole bar to a drink, I just want a glass of wine."

"That is the price for a glass."

"Do I get to keep the glass?"

The two patrons waiting to be served had been joined by another couple of patrons. The barman turned to them and said, "Sorry for the wait, I'll be right with you."

"No hurry," said one of customers "we want to see what wine you finally sell him."

The barman looked at me and said, "I will give you a glass of Sancerre for what you would expect to pay for a glass of Mateus."

"Are you sure it's a good wine?"

"It is an excellent wine; you will taste no better."

"Okay, go ahead, pour me a glass."

He poured and left to take care of the waiting patrons.

The first customer said "I would like a bottle of Dom Perignon but I don't want to pay anymore for it than I would pay for a bottle of Blue Nun."

The barman shot me a look, and as he did, I tipped my glass to him and took a sip.

Left to my own devices, I sat there with the lyrics of the Rolling Stones 'Country Honk' running in my head 'I'm sitting in a bar, tipplin a jar in Jackson's'-I looked around but couldn't see any honky-tonk women.

I glanced to my left where between the end of the bar and the wall was the largest table in the wine bar. Chrome and glass of course, but no stools. There were two guys and four women occupying it. When I came in they were quite noisy, but now they were standing in silence staring at me. I looked at them again and one said, "nice job, when we came in that prick was really snooty to us."

"I've come to the conclusion that a wine bar is nothing more than a rubbish pub. Are you American?"

"Yep."

"Where about in America do you come from?"

"We're from all over the States," said one of the females in the group, "there are about 30 of us here on a comparative education course. We'll be here for about three months."

"When did you arrive?"

"We got here Monday. This town is an absolute zoo!"

"Festival's on. In another couple of weeks you'll see a huge difference."

"Trouble is, everything is so crowded that this pisspot wine bar was the only place we could find a table."

"You really want to go to the Festival Club, that's where all the action is centered - great people and a great bar."

"Is it close by?"

"It's right in the center of Edinburgh, just up the hill and around the corner."

"It's not a private club is it?"

"Actually you do need a membership, but if you want, I can get you in."

"Lead on, we're up for it."

We finished our drinks, and as we headed out I gave a cheery wave to the barman.

The walk to the Festival Club took about five minutes and, as usual, the entrance was busy with people arriving and leaving. I said to my group, "just stay close to me and I will lead you in."

We went through the entrance and, as we passed the doormen I flashed my card, pointed at the American group and said "it's okay they're with me."

I carried on through the entrance then a voice from behind me called "just a minute, can I take a look at that card."

I turned to see one of the doormen looking at me with his hand outstretched. "Why do you want to see it again?"

"It doesn't look like a regular membership card," he said.

"Of course it doesn't, it's a special card."

"Just let me take a look at it!"

"I can't, people may see it and that's not allowed."

"Then you and your friends will have to leave."

"That's not very hospitable, they've just arrived from the USA."

"Unless you let me look at that card you can't come in."

I turned to my new group of friends and said "this is very unusual; it looks like we'll have to back out of here."

"No problem," said one of the guys, "it's not the first club we've been turned away from."

One of the girls, whose name I had learned was Lorna said "let's go back to our lodgings, we have a huge common room and lots of beer and wine."

"Sounds great." I said.

We headed for their lodgings which they told me were on Melville Street, a ten-minute walk from where we were. As we walked I thought to myself that trying to get seven people into the Festival Club using a blood donor card was probably stretching it a bit. I should probably get a sheriff star from a toy shop and paste it, and my picture, on the inside.

Chapter 18

The Americans - Part II

The next day I met Ronnie in the pub at lunchtime.

First thing he said was, "Miss pinking shears has not given up one whit in trying to track you down. Flynn is still stoking her fires at every chance he gets, I think your best chance is to leave the country."

I shrugged and said, "if those donkey riders catch sight of you going through Portobello on your way to your flat in Musselburgh your journey will turn into a nightmare. You'll be found on the beach the next morning with only your head sticking up above the sand. You better hope it's a neap tide."

"Better than hearing the sound of snipping pinking shears coming up behind you."

"Screw them all, I met a bunch of new friends last night. They are Americans."

"Where did you meet them?"

"In a wine bar on Castle Street."

"What the hell were you doing in a wine bar?"

"I went in on a whim. You should try it, calming atmosphere, nothing like that big glitzy mirror they have behind the bar in here."

"You can barely see it behind all the bottles, chalkboards and signs they have taped on it!" He said. "Plus, it hasn't been cleaned in probably 40 years."

"Well, apart from the soothing ambience, it had great customers, a fantastic barman who would go well out of his way to make the best drink he could for you, and I've never seen a better selection of beer, liquor, and wine."

"Sounds good, I'm meeting Sydney this afternoon. We'll definitely go there and have a few brews, but what did you say about meeting Americans?"

"You're meeting Psycho Syd?!?"

"He's not as bad as you tend to make him out."

"Not as bad! Do you remember Caroline Allen's wedding? He didn't even make it through the church vestibule. He stood there claiming that he had shagged not only the bride but all four of the bridesmaids. Finally, a bridesmaid's boyfriend hit him and the brouhaha was on. It took four ushers to throw him out the door. They had to bolt it to keep him out. He was banging and kicking on it for 10 minutes before the police arrived and arrested him."

"Anyway, what were you saying about the Americans?"

"They're here for a few months doing international education studies. I think they're taking classes at Edinburgh University and teaching in various schools around the city. There's 30 of them staying in a large rooming house on Melville Street. The ground floor has a great big common room and we sat around drinking beer and playing music. It's very close to the 'Auld Hoose' pub and we're all meeting there tonight."

"Are they all-male?"

"Only about three. I seemed to hit it off with a girl called Lorna."

"What time are you meeting them?"

"Seven."

He glanced at his watch. "I have to go and meet Syd, we'll definitely go to the wine bar. See you at seven."

With that we split up.

I arrived at the "Auld Hoose" a little before seven and sat down at a table. It was an old style establishment. There were no windows and the entire pub, including the floor, barstools, tables, walls and the bar itself were made from a very dark wood. The lighting was practically nonexistent. Compared to the wine bar it was night and day.

Its most striking feature stood in the center of the pub. It was a fake tree trunk about three feet wide, slightly at an angle and gnarled like a real tree. This tree came through the floor, and just where the branches began, disappeared into the ceiling. In this a dimly lit environment you could almost believe it was a real tree. Why anyone would want a real tree growing through the roof of their house was where disbelief set in.

Ronnie arrived and sat down at my table.

"What the fuck! That wine bar was nothing like you told me. When we went in I thought my eyes had just been dilated. The most pompous prick in the bartending industry was behind the bar. He claimed he had none of the drinks we tried to order.

When, for the third time, he told us to go outside and look at the sign above the door, Syd grabbed his tie and dragged him across the bar."

"So what did you do?"

"I could see nothing good was going to come of this, so I hot-footed it out of there."

"Strange, it must be different in the evening."

At that point the Americans started streaming through the door, their eyes squinting as they tried to see in the dimly lit atmosphere. I stood up and waved my arms crosswise above my head to attract their attention.

They all trooped over to us.

"Wow what a cool place," said one of them. "Nothing like that shitty wine bar with the asshole barman."

"What do you mean?" Ronnie asked her.

"Sorry." I quickly interjected. "This is my friend Ronnie. I'll let you introduce yourselves."

"We're getting used to the no waitress, no tipping manner of the Scottish pubs," said one of the Americans. "We'll head up to the bar and get a round in. What can we get you two?"

"Thank you, we'll have a couple of pints of lager," I responded.

As they headed towards the bar Ronnie turned to me and said "What did she mean by shitty wine bar?"

"I don't know. I think they're used to a better level of service in America."

The "Auld Hoose" is a very warm and friendly place to spend an evening. Everyone enjoyed themselves and I spent most of the evening chatting with Lorna. When closing time arrived Lorna and I made a date to see each other again.

I could not know it at the time, but that evening I had met my future wife.

The Americans rooming house was temporary housing. After a few weeks the group broke up to move to separate accommodations. Some went to live with host families for another few weeks and others rented flats.

Lorna and I had been dating during this period. She and two other girls had rented a house.

"It's great!" she told me, "right on the beach."

Most Americans I had met seemed to aspire to having a home on the beach. Not so much for the Scots. Lorna had never spent an autumn, a winter and a spring in Scotland.

The day after she moved into the house I went over to see her. The house was indeed on the beach, Portobello beach.

As I stood in front of the house to my left I could see where the rented donkeys were led around in circles, and to my right I could see the seafront of Musselburgh. While I'm here, I thought, I will just spend all of my time inside the house.

In October Lorna and her roommates had a party at the so called 'beach house'. All the Americans were there plus many new people they had met. I had invited my three amigos Anton, Rainer and Dick. It was a great party with the music cranked up and the booze flowing freely. Every light was on and all through the house the attendees were having a great time.

I had set myself up next to the record player and was making sure of a steady selection of good dancing music. My three amigos were working the single ladies throughout the rest of the house.

From my corner I noticed an American girl I had seen a few times in the Auld Hoose. In the pub she usually wore a scarf over her blonde hair and was always smiling and very friendly. She was standing in the opposite corner of the room and out of the corner of my eye I saw her making her way towards me.

She came over and stood in front of me and asked "why do you keep playing the same record over and over?"

"Because I like it, and no one seems to be complaining or even noticing."

She smiled and said "I'm Kathy."

"I'm RJ. I've seen you in the Auld Hoose a couple of times."

The record had finished and I turned to put the needle back to the beginning. When I turned back she was still standing there. I asked her if she wanted to dance and she seemed quite keen. We danced a couple of times and then went to get some beer.

"Aren't you Lorna's boyfriend?" she asked.

"Sort of, our relationship's pretty loose; in fact, I don't think I've seen her all evening."

We talked for the rest of the evening and as the party began to break up I asked her if she would like to get together with me the following evening.

She said "sure" and we arranged to meet the following night in the center of Edinburgh at a bar called the Beer and Bite.

We met and I found out she was staying with a host family in an area of Edinburgh called Colinton. By remarkable coincidence I was playing football the following morning in Colinton. I explained how to get to the field and we agreed to meet at the game. She didn't seem to have any interest in football as she sat on the sideline reading a book. After the game we went for a beer and she explained she was looking for a flat in the city.

We began seeing each other on a regular basis and she did indeed find a flat in the center of Edinburgh. It was an old tenement style building with her flat on the fourth floor. She shared it with three other guys. I spent some time there and thought of it as a rather a run-down dump. My flat was also close to the city center and she seemed to prefer spending more time there than at her place.

One day came a knock at my door and standing there was Kathy. She had tears in her eyes as she explained to me that the ceiling in her room had become so waterlogged from the plumbing renovations in the flat above that it collapsed. Her room was now a wet plaster covered disaster and unfit for anybody to live in.

"I have nowhere to stay" she said.

"Come on in, you can stay here."

She picked up her suitcase and came on in.

No longer would my life ever be the same.

The following is an excerpt from the next book in the series.

The Dishwasher

We had moved from Michigan and were now living in Massachusetts. Kathy, for some reason which escapes me now, had to go back to Michigan for a few days. I was left in charge of our two young children.

After a couple of days our dishwasher, which was empty when Kathy left, was now full of dirty dishes. Strange as it may seem, I had gotten to this stage of my life and had never operated a dishwasher. If it had just landed from outer space I would have no more idea on how to use it.

I decided to wing it.

After studying the dials on top of the door I began to understand how to turn it on. Inside the door were little lidded cups where you poured the dishwashing liquid.

I grabbed the dishwashing liquid from the back of the sink and poured it in the cup in the door. For good measure I also poured some in the cup that said extra rinse and closed the lids and the door. I then set the dials on top to what I figured were the appropriate settings and turned it on. Things began to happen, I heard water pouring in and then the familiar swishing sound. Everything appeared to be just fine.

I stayed in the kitchen making some lunch.

A few minutes later the dishwasher began its attack.

I glanced over, big wet bubbles were pouring from all four sides of its door and advancing across the floor towards me. I stepped through the bubbles and switched it off.

My five-year-old son came into the kitchen, looked at the mass of bubbles and said, "Wow Dad, I've never seen Mom do this."

"I don't know why it is doing this, I'll get a bucket and mop."

I sopped the bubbly water up, then took a look inside the dishwasher. The bubbles had subsided. With everything seeming to be in order I restarted it. Within a few seconds the attack of the bubbles resumed.

"Hey Samantha," my son called "you have to see this!"

Within a few seconds my two-year-old daughter appeared. "Dad this is great!" she exclaimed while clapping her hands and jumping up and down.

I switched it off again and thought, this is going to take all day.

I then had a great idea.

I went down to the garage and got the shop-vac. I brought it up to the kitchen, plugged it in and re-started the dishwasher. As the watery bubbles began pouring out, I used the shop-vac to suck it up while it was still on the door.

When the shop-vac was full I took it outside and poured the bubbly mess onto the driveway. Our driveway, although fairly short, had a nice slope. I had found the ideal way to get rid of the mess.

I repeated this process a couple of more times. On the fourth trip I found my children having a great time rolling around in the bubbles on the driveway. Seeing they were nicely occupied I carried on with the task at hand.

We lived in an area where the surrounding houses all had very young children. As I made more trips I found more children rolling around in the bubbly foam. Nothing I could really do about it, so I just let them play.

After a couple of more trips we seemed to have every child in the neighborhood playing in our driveway. Their mothers were also gathering and were not too happy.

"What the hell are you doing! My Annie is soaking wet!"

"My dishwasher has gone berserk and is spewing this bubbly foam everywhere."

"Our children are playing in dirty dishwashing water!" exclaimed another mother.

"I don't think is dirty, it's just a whole bunch of watery bubbles that keeps pouring out from all around the door."

"What did you use for soap?"

"Dishwashing liquid, I may have used too much."

"You're an idiot. You use dishwasher soap not dishwashing liquid in a dishwasher."

They started to wade into the bubbles to collect their children. This was more difficult than it seemed. First they had to try and identify which child was theirs, and then trying to grab a slippery child which doesn't want to go anywhere proved almost impossible.

"When does Kathy get back?" asked our next-door neighbor.

"Soon."

About the Author

Born and raised in Scotland, RJ moved to the
United States after marriage and lives in
Massachusetts with his wife Kathy along with their
three children.

He is currently working on his next two
books about his adventures as a corporate executive
and entrepreneur in America.

ONE LAST THING... Thanks for reading! If you want to make comments on this book I would be very grateful if you'd post a short review on Amazon. Your opinion really does make a difference.

You can leave a review for this book on Amazon at www.amazon.com. Thanks again for your support!